Colorado Academic Standards, Social Studies

Colorado. Dept. of Education. Office of Standards and Assessment

Improving
Academic
Achievement

Colorado Academic
S T A N D A R D S

Social Studies

Overview of Changes
Social Studies Standards

Principles of the Standards Review Process

The Colorado Model Content Standards revision process was informed by these guiding principles:

- Begin with the end in mind; define what prepared graduates need in order to be successful using 21st century skills in our global economy.
- Align K-12 standards with early childhood expectations and higher education.
- Change is necessary.
- Standards will be deliberately designed for clarity, rigor, and coherence.
- There will be fewer, higher and clearer standards.
- Standards will be actionable.

Notable Changes to the Colorado Model Content Standards in History, Geography, Economics, and Civics

The most evident changes to the Colorado standards are replacing grade-band expectations (K-4, 5-8, and 9-12) with grade-level specific expectations. These are explained here in addition to other changes that are apparent upon comparison between the current social studies standards and the proposed changes.

1. Impact of standards articulation by grade level. The original Colorado Model Content Standards for history, geography, civics, and economics were designed to provide districts with benchmarks of learning at grades 4, 8, and 12. The standards revision subcommittee was charged with providing more a specific learning trajectory of concepts and skills across grade levels, from early school readiness to postsecondary preparedness. Articulating standards by grade level in each area affords greater specificity (clearer standards) in describing the learning path across levels (higher standards), while focusing on a few key ideas at each grade level (fewer standards).

2. Articulation of high school standards. High school standards are not articulated by grade level, but by standard. . This is intended to support district decisions about how best to design curriculum and courses- whether through an integrated approach, a traditional course sequence, or h alternative approaches such as career and technical education. The high school standards delineate what all high school students should know and be able to do in order to be well prepared for any postsecondary option. The individual standards are not meant to represent a course or a particular timeframe. All high school students should be able to reach these rigorous standards within four years.

3. Integration of P-2 Council's recommendations. The subcommittees integrated the P-2 building blocks document into the P-12 standards, aligning expectations to a great degree. Important concepts and skills are defined clearly across these foundational years, detailing expectations to a much greater extent for teachers and parents.

4. Standards are written for mastery. The proposed revisions to standards define mastery of concepts and skills. Mastery means that a student has facility with a skill or concept in multiple contexts. This is not an indication that instruction at a grade-level expectation begins and only occurs at that grade level. Maintenance of previously mastered concepts and skills and scaffolding future learning are the domain of curriculum and instruction— not standards.

5. Intentional integration of technology use, most notably at the high school level. Using appropriate technology allows students access to concepts and skills in ways that mirror the 21st century workplace.

6. Intentional opportunities for integration. The subcommittees in history, geography, civics, and economics worked within content area and also within multi-content area grade level groups. The social studies standards were created to intentionally encourage integration. In addition, the subcommittees were focused on the consolidation of standards.

7. Intentional integration of personal financial literacy. Personal financial literacy was integrated P-13 in the economics standards in order to ensure the school experience prepared students for the financial expectations that await them on leaving school. Personal financial literacy expectations are indicated as (PFL) within the document and the content focuses on: goal setting and financial responsibility; income and career; planning, saving, and investing; using credit; and risk management and insurance. The mathematics standards were also intentionally integrated with personal financial literacy.

Below is a quick guide to changes in the social studies standards:

Area	Summary of changes	
	Current Standards	Proposed Revisions
Number of standards	Separate standards.	The proposal is to combine and create 4 standards in social studies.
Names of standards	History: 1. Chronology 2. Historical Inquiry 3. Societies are diverse 4. Science, technology, economic activity 5. Political institutions and theories 6. Religious and philosophical ideas Geography: 1. Geographic Tools 2. Place and Region 3. Physical processes 4. Economic, political, cultural, and social processes 5. Human and environment interaction 6. People, places, and environments to understand past, present and plan for future Economics: 1. Scarcity 2. Production & Distribution 3. Trade, exchange and interdependence Civics: 1. Purpose of government and constitutional principles 2. Structure and function of government 3. Political relationships 4. Roles, rights and responsibilities of citizens	Standard 1. History: History develops moral understanding, defines identity and creates an appreciation of how things change while building skills in judgment and decision-making. History enhances the ability to read varied sources and develop the skills to analyze, interpret, and communicate. Standard 2. Geography: Geography provides students with an understanding of spatial perspectives and technologies for spatial analysis, awareness of interdependence of world regions and resources and how places are connected on local, national and global scales. Standard 3. Economics: Economics teaches a student how society manages its scarce resources, how people make decisions, how people interact in the domestic and international markets, and how forces and trends affect the economy as a whole. Personal financial literacy applies the economic way of thinking to help individuals understand how to manage their own scarce resources using a logical decision-making process of prioritization based on analysis of the costs and benefits of every choice. Standard 4. Civics: Civics teaches students the complexity of the origins, structure, and functions, of governments; the rights, roles and responsibilities of ethical citizenship; the importance of law; and the skills necessary to participate in all levels of government.
Integration of 21st century and postsecondary workforce readiness skills	• Not deliberately addressed in original document.	• A design feature of the revision process. • Intentionally integrated into evidence outcomes.
P-2	• Standards articulated for grade band beginning with kindergarten. • Benchmarks articulated by grade band of K-4, with most geared to upper grades.	• Pre-K included. • Grade level expectations articulated for each elementary grade level. • Clear expectations articulated for grades P-2.
Number of grade level expectations	• Average of 27 benchmarks per grade level.	• Average of 10 grade level expectations per grade level (P-8), with 17 for high school.

Social Studies Subcommittee Members

Co-Chairs:

Ms. Peggy Altoff (Geography)
District
Social Studies Facilitator
Colorado Springs District 11
Colorado Springs

Dr. Fritz Fischer (History)
Higher Education
Professor of History
University of Northern Colorado
Niwot

Subcommittee Members:

History

Mr. Ben DeGrow
Business
Education Policy Analyst
Independence Institute
Arvada

Ms. Amanda Prichard
Middle School
Teacher
Jefferson County Public Schools
Littleton

Mr. Chris Elnicki
District
Social Studies Coordinator
Cherry Creek School District
Centennial

Ms. Lynn Stumbras-Ritchie
Middle School
Middle School Teacher, Retired
Littleton

Ms. Abbie Martin
Middle School
Middle School Teacher
Adams 12 School District
Thornton

Ms. Virginia Lindeman-Roman
District
Curriculum Content Specialist
Littleton

Ms. Deborah Pearce
High School
Secondary Teacher Jefferson County Public
Schools
Arvada

Ms. Elma Ruiz
District
Elementary Social Studies Coordinator
Denver Public Schools
Denver

Michelle Pearson
Middle School
Department Chair, Hulstrom Options School
Adams 12 School District
Broomfield

Dr. Katherine L. Sturdevant
Higher Education
Professor of History
Pikes Peak Community College
Colorado Springs

Geography

Ms. Lacey Alkire
District
Secondary Content Specialist
Jefferson County Public Schools
Lakewood

Dr. James M. Dunn
Higher Education
Assistant Professor of Geography
University of Colorado
Greeley

Ms. Loree Eatherson
Elementary School
Teacher
Cherry Creek School District
Aurora

Ms. Judith Hansen
Elementary School
Jefferson County School District
Retired
Littleton

Ms. Jane Houssiere
Middle School
Teacher
Adams County School District
Boulder

Ms. Marianne Kenney
District
Social Studies Instructional Specialist
Denver Public Schools
Denver

Ms. Teri LeFabre
High School
High School GVC Specialist
Mesa School District
Grand Junction

Ms. Katie Navin
Business
Program Coordinator
Colorado Alliance for Environmental
Education
Lakewood

Ms. Renee Sward
Elementary School
Teacher
Academy School District 20
Colorado Springs

Dr. Rebecca Theobald
Higher Education
Assistant Adjoint Professor of Geography
University of Colorado at Colorado Springs
Colorado Springs

Economics

Mr. Peter Berstien
Parent
Vice President of Private Banking
Bank of the West
Denver

Ms. Tracey Boychuk
High School
Teacher
Jefferson County Public Schools
Broomfield

Ms. Stacy Brophy
Business
Vice President
D&S Partnerships
Eckley

Ms. Tammy Durnford
Business
Manager of Client Relations
Sharkey, Howes & Javer, Inc.
Denver

Michael Goodman, J.D.
High School
Teacher and Department Chair
Cherry Creek School District
Centennial

Donald Taylor
High School
Teacher
Colorado Springs District 11
Colorado Springs

Mr. Fred Wilson
High School
Teacher
Cherry Creek School District
Berthoud

Mr. Michael Wolf
Business
Project Engineer
FedEx Express
Aurora

Ms. Teresa Yohon
Higher Education
Research Scientist
Colorado State University
Fort Collins

Civics

Mr. John Crone
Business
President
Clearbrook Consulting Group
Dillon

Dr. Lisa Bardwell
Business
Chief Executive Officer
Earth Force
Denver

Ms. Gloria Hader
Preschool
Instructional Coach
Jefferson County Public Schools
Evergreen

Ms. Christina Jean
High School
Social Studies Department Chair
Boulder Valley School District
Boulder

Mr. Richard T. Law
Middle School Principal
Colorado Springs District 11
Colorado Springs

Dr. Brian Loney
District
K-12 Social Studies Coordinator
Jefferson County Public Schools
Denver

Justin Prochnow, J.D.
Business
Associate Attorney
Law Firm of Greenberg Traurig
Denver

Mr. Darik Williams
Elementary School
Assistant Principal
Cherry Creek School District
Denver

Mr. Kent Willmann
High School
Teacher
St. Vrain School District
Longmont

Ms. Sarah Wilson
Higher Education
PhD Candidate
University of Northern Colorado
Greeley

Dr. Kaylah Zelig
Higher Education
Professor, Political Science & Business
Community College of Denver
Louisville

Mrs. Ann Wolfe
Parent
Volunteer
Cherry Creek School District
Aurora

Personal Financial Literacy Subcommittee

Ms. Joan Andersen
Higher Education
Chair of Economics and Investments
Colorado Community College System
Faculty, Arapahoe Community College
Centennial

Ms. Deann Bucher
District
Social Studies Coordinator
Boulder Valley School District
Boulder

Ms. Pam Cummings
High School
Secondary High School Teacher
Jefferson County Public Schools
Littleton

Ms. Annetta J. Gallegos
District
Career and Technical Education
Denver Public Schools
Denver

Dr. Jack L. Gallegos
High School
Teacher
Englewood High School
Englewood

Ms. Dora Gonzales
Higher Education
Field Supervisor/Instructor
Alternative Licensure Program
Pikes Peak BOCES
Colorado Springs

Mr. Richard Martinez, Jr.
Business
President and CEO
Young Americans Center for Financial
Education and Young Americans Bank
Denver

Ms. Julie McLean
Business
Director of Financial Education
Arapahoe Credit Union
Arvada

Ms. Linda Motz
High School
Family and Consumer Sciences Teacher
Palisade High School
Grand Junction

Ms. Patti (Rish) Ord
High School
Business Teacher and Department
Coordinator
Overland High School
Aurora

Mr. R. Bruce Potter, CFP®
Business
President, Potter Financial Solutions, Inc.
Westminster

Mr. Ted Seiler
District
Career and Technical Education Coordinator
Cherry Creek School District
Greenwood Village

Mr. Tim Taylor
Business
President
Colorado Succeeds
Denver

Ms. Elizabeth L. Whitham
Higher Education
Business and Economics Faculty
Lamar Community College
Lamar

Ms. Robin Wise
Business
President and CEO
Junior Achievement – Rocky Mountain, Inc.
Denver

Ms. Coni S. Wolfe
High School
Business Department Chairperson
Mesa County Valley School District
Palisade

Social Studies National Expert Reviewer

Dr. Mary A. McFarland

Dr. Mary A. McFarland, a past president of the National Council for the Social Studies, has also served as director of social studies, K–12 and director of professional development for a suburban school district in St. Louis County, MO. She has taught at elementary, high school, and university levels, and is currently a full-time curriculum developer, researcher, and educational consultant. Recent projects include authoring Internet curriculum for a 32-volume social studies video library on teaching and learning, and serving as the facilitator for eight video workshops on the use of the library—videos sponsored by NCSS/Annenberg and produced by WGBH-Boston.

McFarland has served as a curriculum consultant for the states of Maine and Maryland and worked on the task force for development of the National Council for the Social Studies Curriculum Standards, *Expectations of Excellence*, and has co-authored a social studies textbook series. She has presented workshop sessions and institutes at the Library of Congress, the National Archives, the Smithsonian Institution, Harvard University, and in Latvia, Japan, Germany, South Korea, and Canada as well as throughout the United States. Mary continues to work with educators and administrators in several states across all curriculum areas and levels of education; serves on the faculty at Harvard summer institutes; and serves as instructor for WIDE World Online Professional Development courses, developed at the Harvard Graduate School of Education.

References

The social studies subcommittees used a variety of resources representing a broad range of perspectives to inform their work. Those references include:

- Singapore National Curriculum
- Massachusetts Curriculum Framework
- Indiana Department of Education
- Finland – National Core Curriculum
- WestEd Colorado Model Content Standards Review
- Building Blocks to the Colorado K-12 Content Standards

Colorado Academic Standards
Social Studies Standards

"Teaching social studies powerfully and authentically begins with a deep knowledge and understanding of the subject and its unique goals. Social studies programs prepare students to identify, understand, and work to solve the challenges facing our diverse nation in an increasingly interdependent world. Education for citizenship should help students acquire and learn to use the skills, knowledge, and attitudes that will prepare them to be competent and responsible citizens throughout their lives. Competent and responsible citizens are informed and thoughtful, participate in their communities, are involved politically, and exhibit moral and civic virtues."

A Vision of Powerful Teaching and Learning in the Social Studies:
Building Social Understanding and Civic Efficacy (NCSS, 2008)

~ ~

Preparing students for the 21st century cannot be accomplished without a strong and sustaining emphasis on the social studies. The social studies provide cornerstone skills that are the key to opening doors for a more diverse, competitive workforce and responsible citizenry. Students use critical thinking, self-assessment, reasoning, problem-solving, collaboration, research, and investigation to make connections in new and innovative ways as they progress through social studies education. These standards outline the knowledge and skills needed to help young people develop the ability to make informed and reasoned decisions for the public good as citizens of a culturally diverse, democratic society in an interdependent world.

Social studies is essential to understanding the complexity of the world. It provides the context and understanding of how humans interact with each other and with the environment over time. It offers the crucial knowledge needed to create a framework for understanding the systems of society.

Colorado's social studies standards lay out a vision of these vitally important disciplines and describe what all students should know and be able to do at each grade level through eighth grade, and through high school. The authors of this document are educators in preschool through twelfth grade, higher education professors, business and military representatives, and community members. The group developed a set of competencies starting with "the end in mind." What concepts and skills would a "prepared graduate" in the 21st century possess after completing high school? The answers to this question framed the work that led to the development of four standards in social studies for grades P-12.

Standards Organization and Construction

As the subcommittee began the revision process to improve the existing standards, it became evident that the way the standards information was organized, defined, and constructed needed to change from the existing documents. The new design is intended to provide more clarity and direction for teachers, and to show how 21st century skills and the elements of school readiness and postsecondary and workforce readiness indicators give depth and context to essential learning.

The "Continuum of State Standards Definitions" section that follows shows the hierarchical order of the standards components. The "Standards Template" section demonstrates how this continuum is put into practice.

The elements of the revised standards are:

Prepared Graduate Competencies: The preschool through twelfth-grade concepts and skills that all students who complete the Colorado education system must master to ensure their success in a postsecondary and workforce setting.

Standard: The topical organization of an academic content area.

High School Expectations: The articulation of the concepts and skills of a standard that indicates a student is making progress toward being a prepared graduate. *What do students need to know in high school?*

Grade Level Expectations: The articulation (at each grade level), concepts, and skills of a standard that indicate a student is making progress toward being ready for high school. *What do students need to know from preschool through eighth grade?*

Evidence Outcomes: The indication that a student is meeting an expectation at the mastery level. *How do we know that a student can do it?*

21st Century Skills and Readiness Competencies: Includes the following:

> *Inquiry Questions:*
> Sample questions are intended to promote deeper thinking, reflection and refined understandings precisely related to the grade level expectation.

> *Relevance and Application:*
> Examples of how the grade level expectation is applied at home, on the job or in a real-world, relevant context.

> *Nature of the Discipline:*
> The characteristics and viewpoint one keeps as a result of mastering the grade level expectation.

Continuum of State Standards Definitions

Prepared Graduate Competency

Prepared graduate competencies are the P-12 concepts and skills that all students who complete the Colorado education system must master to ensure their success in a postsecondary and workforce setting.

Standards

Standards are the topical organization of an academic content area.

P-8   High School

Grade Level Expectations

Expectations articulate at each grade level the knowledge and skills that indicate a student is making progress toward being ready for high school.

What do students need to know?

High School Expectations

Expectations articulate the knowledge and skills that indicate a student is making progress toward being a prepared graduate.

What do students need to know?

Evidence Outcomes

Evidence outcomes are the indication that a student is meeting an expectation at the mastery level.

How do we know that a student can do it?

21st Century and PWR Skills

Inquiry Questions:
Sample questions intended to promote deeper thinking, reflection and refined understandings precisely related to the grade level expectation.
Relevance and Application:
Examples of how the grade level expectation is applied at home, on the job or in a real-world, relevant context.
Nature of the Discipline:
The characteristics and viewpoint one keeps as a result of mastering the grade level expectation.

Evidence Outcomes

Evidence outcomes are the indication that a student is meeting an expectation at the mastery level.

How do we know that a student can do it?

21st Century and PWR Skills

Inquiry Questions:
Sample questions intended to promote deeper thinking, reflection and refined understandings precisely related to the grade level expectation.
Relevance and Application:
Examples of how the grade level expectation is applied at home, on the job or in a real-world, relevant context.
Nature of the Discipline:
The characteristics and viewpoint one keeps as a result of mastering the grade level expectation.

Content Area: **NAME OF CONTENT AREA**
Standard: The topical organization of an academic content area.

Prepared Graduates:
➢ The P-12 concepts and skills that all students who complete the Colorado education system must master to ensure their success in a postsecondary and workforce setting

High School and Grade Level Expectations

Concepts and skills students master:

High School Expectations: The articulation of the concepts and skills that indicate a student is making progress toward being a prepared graduate.

Grade Level Expectations: The articulation at each grade level of the concepts and skills that indicate a student is making progress toward being ready for high school.

What do students need to know?

Evidence Outcomes	21st Century Skills and Readiness Competencies
Students can:	Inquiry Questions:
Evidence outcomes are the indication that a student is meeting an expectation at the mastery level.	Sample questions intended to promote deeper thinking, reflection and refined understandings precisely related to the grade level expectation.
How do we know that a student can do it?	Relevance and Application:
	Examples of how the grade level expectation is applied at home, on the job or in a real-world, relevant context.
	Nature of the Discipline:
	The characteristics and viewpoint one keeps as a result of mastering the grade level expectation.

Prepared Graduate Competencies in Social Studies

The prepared graduate competencies are the preschool through twelfth-grade concepts and skills that all students who complete the Colorado education system must master to ensure their success in a postsecondary and workforce setting.

Prepared graduates in social studies:
1. Use the tools, thinking, and practices of history, geography, economics, and civics to:
   a. Solve problems, make decisions and analyze issues from multiple perspectives as a responsible member of society
   b. Read, write, and communicate ideas

Prepared graduates in history:
1. Develop an understanding of how people view, construct, and interpret history
2. Analyze key historical periods and patterns of change over time within and across nations and cultures

Prepared graduates in geography:
1. Develop spatial understanding, perspectives, and personal connections to the world
2. Examine places and regions and the connections among them

Prepared graduates in economics:
1. Understand the allocation of scarce resources in societies through analysis of individual choice, market interaction, and public policy
2. Acquire the knowledge and economic reasoning skills to make sound financial decisions (PFL)

Prepared graduates in civics:
1. Analyze and practice rights, roles, and responsibilities of citizens
2. Analyze the origins, structure, and functions of governments and their impacts on societies and citizens

Colorado Academic Standards
Social Studies

Standards are the topical organization of an academic content area. The four standards of social studies are:

1. History
   History develops moral understanding, defines identity and creates an appreciation of how things change while building skills in judgment and decision-making. History enhances the ability to read varied sources and develop the skills to analyze, interpret and communicate.

2. Geography
   Geography provides students with an understanding of spatial perspectives and technologies for spatial analysis, awareness of interdependence of world regions and resources and how places are connected at local, national and global scales.

3. Economics
   Economics teaches how society manages its scarce resources, how people make decisions, how people interact in the domestic and international markets, and how forces and trends affect the economy as a whole. Personal financial literacy applies the economic way of thinking to help individuals understand how to manage their own scarce resources using a logical decision-making process of prioritization based on analysis of the costs and benefits of every choice.

4. Civics
   Civics teaches the complexity of the origins, structure, and functions of governments; the rights, roles and responsibilities of ethical citizenship; the importance of law; and the skills necessary to participate in all levels of government.

Social Studies
Grade Level Expectations at a Glance

Standard	Grade Level Expectation
High School	
1. History	1. The historical method of inquiry to ask questions, evaluate primary and secondary sources, critically analyze and interpret data, and develop interpretations defended by evidence from a variety of primary and secondary sources 2. Analyze the key concepts of continuity and change, cause and effect, complexity, unity and diversity over time 3. The significance of ideas as powerful forces throughout history
2. Geography	1. Use different types of maps and geographic tools to analyze features on Earth to investigate and solve geographic questions 2. Explain and interpret geographic variables that influence the interaction of people, places, and environments 3. The interconnected nature of the world, its people and places
3. Economics	1. Productive resources - natural, human, capital - are scarce; therefore choices are made about how individuals, businesses, governments, and societies allocate these resources 2. Economic policies impact markets 3. Government and competition impact markets 4. Design, analyze, and apply a financial plan based on short- and long-term financial goals (PFL) 5. Analyze strategic spending, saving, and investment options to achieve the objectives of diversification, liquidity, income, and growth (PFL) 6. The components of personal credit to manage credit and debt (PFL) 7. Identify, develop, and evaluate risk-management strategies (PFL)
4. Civics	1. Research, formulate positions, and engage in appropriate civic participation to address local, state, or national issues or policies 2. Purposes of and limitations on the foundations, structures and functions of government 3. Analyze how public policy - domestic and foreign - is developed at the local, state, and national levels and compare how policy-making occurs in other forms of government
Eighth Grade	
1. History	1. Formulate appropriate hypotheses about United States history based on a variety of historical sources and perspectives 2. The historical eras, individuals, groups, ideas and themes from the origins of the American Revolution through Reconstruction and their relationships with one another
2. Geography	1. Use geographic tools to analyze patterns in human and physical systems 2. Conflict and cooperation occur over space and resources
3. Economics	1. Economic freedom, including free trade, is important for economic growth 2. Manage personal credit and debt(PFL)
4. Civics	1. Analyze elements of continuity and change in the United States government and the role of citizens over time 2. The place of law in a constitutional system

Social Studies
Grade Level Expectations at a Glance

Standard	Grade Level Expectation
Seventh Grade	
1. History	1. Seek and evaluate multiple historical sources with different points of view to investigate a historical question and to formulate and defend a thesis with evidence 2. The historical eras, individuals, groups, ideas and themes within regions of the Eastern Hemisphere and their relationships with one another
2. Geography	1. Use geographic tools to gather data and make geographic inferences and predictions 2. Regions have different issues and perspectives
3. Economics	1. Supply and demand influence price and profit in a market economy 2. Manage personal credit and debt (PFL)
4. Civics	1. The different forms of government and international organizations and their influence in the world community 2. Compare how various nations define the rights, responsibilities and roles of citizens
Sixth Grade	
1. History	1. Analyze and interpret historical sources to ask and research historical questions 2. The historical eras, individuals, groups, ideas and themes in regions of the Western Hemisphere and their relationships with one another
2. Geography	1. Use geographic tools to solve problems 2. Human and physical systems vary and interact
3. Economics	1. Identify and analyze different economic systems 2. Saving and investing are key contributors to financial well being (PFL)
4. Civics	1. Analyze the interconnected nature of the United States to other nations 2. Compare multiple systems of governments
Fifth Grade	
1. History	1. Analyze historical sources from multiple points of view to develop an understanding of historical context 2. The historical eras, individuals, groups, ideas, and themes in North America from 1491 through the founding of the United States government
2. Geography	1. Use various geographic tools and sources to answer questions about the geography of the United States 2. Causes and consequences of movement
3. Economics	1. Government and market structures influence financial institutions 2. Utilizing financial institutions to manage personal finances (PFL)
4. Civics	1. The foundations of citizenship in the United States 2. The origins, structure, and functions of the United States government

Social Studies
Grade Level Expectations at a Glance

Standard	Grade Level Expectation
Fourth Grade	
1. History	1. Organize a sequence of events to understand the concepts of chronology and cause and effect in the history of Colorado 2. The historical eras, individuals, groups, ideas, and themes in Colorado history and their relationships to key events in the United States
2. Geography	1. Use several types of geographic tools to answer questions about the geography of Colorado 2. Connections within and across human and physical systems are developed
3. Economics	1. People responded to positive and negative incentives 2. The relationship between choice and opportunity cost (PFL)
4. Civics	1. Analyze and debate multiple perspectives on an issue 2. The origins, structure, and functions of the Colorado government
Third Grade	
1. History	1. Use a variety of sources to distinguish historical fact from fiction 2. People in the past influenced the development and interaction of different communities and regions
2. Geography	1. Use various types of geographic tools to develop spatial thinking 2. The concept of regions is developed through an understanding of similarities and differences in places
3. Economics	1. Describe producers and consumers and how goods and services are exchanged 2. Describe how to meet short-term financial goals (PFL)
4. Civics	1. Respecting the views and rights of others as components of a democratic society 2. The origin, structure and function of local government
Second Grade	
1. History	1. Identify historical sources and utilize the tools of a historian 2. People in the past influenced the history of neighborhoods and communities
2. Geography	1. Use geographic terms and tools to describe space and place 2. People in communities manage, modify, and depend on their environment
3. Economics	1. The scarcity of resources affects the choices of individuals and communities 2. Apply decision-making processes to financial decision making(PFL)
4. Civics	1. Responsible community members advocate for their ideas 2. People use multiple ways to resolve conflicts or differences

Social Studies
Grade Level Expectations at a Glance

Standard	Grade Level Expectation
First Grade	
1. History	1. Describe patterns and chronological order of events of the recent past
	2. Family and cultural traditions in the United States in the past
2. Geography	1. Geographic tools such as maps and globes to represent places
	2. People in different groups and communities interact with each other and the environment
3. Economics	1. People work at different types of jobs and in different types of organizations in order to produce goods and services and receive an income
	2. Identify short term financial goals (PFL)
4. Civics	1. Effective groups have responsible leaders and team members
	2. Notable people, places, holidays and patriotic symbols
Kindergarten	
1. History	1. Ask questions, share information and discuss ideas about the past
	2. The first component in the concept of chronology is to place information in sequential order
2. Geography	1. People belong to different groups and live in different settings around the world that can be found on a map or globe
3. Economics	1. Ownership as a component of economics
	2. Discuss how purchases can be made to meet wants and needs (PFL)
4. Civics	1. Participate in making decisions using democratic traditions
	2. Civic participation takes place in multiple groups
Preschool	
1. History	1. Change and sequence over time
2. Geography	1. Develop spatial understanding, perspectives, and connections to the world
3. Economics	1. People work to meet wants
	2. Recognize money and identify its purpose (PFL)
4. Civics	1. Individuals have unique talents but also work with others in groups
	2. Rules and their purpose in allowing groups to work effectively

21st Century Skills and Readiness Competencies in Social Studies

The social studies subcommittees embedded 21st century skills, school readiness, and postsecondary and workforce readiness skills into the draft revised standards utilizing descriptions developed by Coloradans and vetted by educators, policymakers, and citizens.

Colorado's description of 21st century skills
The 21st century skills are the synthesis of the essential abilities students must apply in our rapidly changing world. Today's students need a repertoire of knowledge and skills that are more diverse, complex, and integrated than any previous generation. Social studies is inherently demonstrated in each of Colorado 21st century skills, as follows:

Critical Thinking and Reasoning – Social studies is a discipline grounded in critical thinking and reasoning. Doing history, geography, civics and economics involves recognizing patterns and relationships across time and space. Social studies provide the structure that makes it possible to describe patterns that exist in nature and society.

Information Literacy – The disciplines of social studies equip students with tools and mental habits to organize and interpret a multitude of resources. A social studies student with information literacy skills can effectively analyze primary and secondary sources, detect bias, use learning tools, including technology, and clearly communicate thoughts using sound reasoning.

Collaboration – The content areas of social studies involve the give and take of ideas. In the course of understanding social studies, students offer ideas, strategies, solutions, justifications, and proofs for others to evaluate. In turn, the student interprets and evaluates the ideas, strategies, solutions, and justifications of others.

Self-Direction – Understanding social studies requires a productive disposition, curiosity and self-direction. This involves monitoring and assessing one's thinking and persisting to search for patterns, relationships, cause and effect, and an understanding of the events and people throughout time.

Invention – The social studies are a dynamic set of content area disciplines, ever expanding with new ideas and understandings. Invention is the key element as students make and test theories, create and use social studies tools, search for patterns and themes, and make connections among ideas, strategies and solutions.

Colorado's Description for School Readiness
(Adopted by the State Board of Education, December 2008)

School readiness describes both the preparedness of a child to engage in and benefit from learning experiences, and the ability of a school to meet the needs of all students enrolled in publicly funded preschools or kindergartens. School readiness is enhanced when schools, families, and community service providers work collaboratively to ensure that every child is ready for higher levels of learning in academic content.

Colorado's Description of Postsecondary and Workforce Readiness
(Adopted by the State Board of Education, June 2009)

Postsecondary and workforce readiness describes the knowledge, skills, and behaviors essential for high school graduates to be prepared to enter college and the workforce and to compete in the global economy. The description assumes students have developed consistent intellectual growth throughout their high school career as a result of academic work that is increasingly challenging, engaging, and coherent. Postsecondary education and workforce readiness assumes that students are ready and able to demonstrate the following without the need for remediation: Critical thinking and problem-solving; finding and using information/information technology; creativity and innovation; global and cultural awareness; civic responsibility; work ethic; personal responsibility; communication; and collaboration.

How These Skills and Competencies are Embedded in the Revised Standards

Three themes are used to describe these important skills and competencies and are interwoven throughout the standards: *inquiry questions; relevance and application; and the nature of each discipline.* These competencies should not be thought of stand-alone concepts, but should be integrated throughout the curriculum in all grade levels. Just as it is impossible to teach thinking skills to students without the content to think about, it is equally impossible for students to understand the content of a discipline without grappling with complex questions and the investigation of topics.

Inquiry Questions – Inquiry is a multifaceted process requiring students to think and pursue understanding. Inquiry demands that students (a) engage in an active observation and questioning process; (b) investigate to gather evidence; (c) formulate explanations based on evidence; (d) communicate and justify explanations, and; (e) reflect and refine ideas. Inquiry is more than hands-on activities; it requires students to cognitively wrestle with core concepts as they make sense of new ideas.

Relevance and Application – The hallmark of learning a discipline is the ability to apply the knowledge, skills, and concepts in real-world, relevant contexts. Components of this include solving problems, developing, adapting, and refining solutions for the betterment of society. The application of a discipline, including how technology assists or accelerates the work, enables students to more fully appreciate how the mastery of the grade level expectation matters after formal schooling is complete.

Nature of Discipline – The unique advantage of a discipline is the perspective it gives the mind to see the world and situations differently. The characteristics and viewpoint one keeps as a result of mastering the grade level expectation is the nature of the discipline retained in the mind's eye.

1. History

The study of history prepares students to develop critical thinking skills in an effort to explain the human experience through events of the past. Discerning clarity from the jumble of conflicting facts and sources, students get a clearer picture of how individuals, communities, and the world connect, both past and present. History develops moral understanding, defines identity and creates an appreciation of how things change, while building judgment and decision-making skills. History enhances the ability to read varied sources and develop the skills necessary to analyze, interpret, and communicate.

History inspires by exposing students to the wonders and beauty of the past. The historical perspective prepares for an ever-changing future by helping to understand changes in the past. It allows students to gain perspective and develop better judgment by discovering and uncovering the complexity of human beings. This allows students to better understand themselves as individuals and their place in a complex and often confusing society. History provides examples of ethical behavior and the context for change, and illustrates the importance of responsible members of society in both our country and our world.

History is a critical component in the future success of a student in the 21st century world. Inquiry is the central component of historical thinking. Students learn the skills of reading, interpreting and analyzing historical sources and develop the ability to craft a well-constructed and communicated historical argument. History teaches the interpretive, analytical, and critical thinking skills that will allow students to become productive citizens in the future.

Prepared Graduates
The prepared graduate competencies are the preschool through twelfth-grade concepts and skills that all students who complete the Colorado education system must master to ensure their success in a postsecondary and workforce setting.

Prepared Graduate Competencies in the History standards are:

➤ Develop an understanding of how people view, construct, and interpret history

➤ Analyze key historical periods and patterns of change over time within and across nations and cultures

---

Adopted: December 10, 2009

Content Area: Social Studies
Standard: 1. History

Prepared Graduates:
➢ Develop an understanding of how people view, construct, and interpret history

Grade Level Expectation: High School

Concepts and skills students master:
1. Use the historical method of inquiry to ask questions, evaluate primary and secondary sources, critically analyze and interpret data, and develop interpretations defended by evidence

Evidence Outcomes	21st Century Skills and Readiness Competencies
Students can: a. Evaluate a historical source for point of view and historical context b. Gather and analyze historical information, including contradictory data, from a variety of primary and secondary sources, including sources located on the Internet, to support or reject hypotheses c. Construct and defend a written historical argument using relevant primary and secondary sources as evidence d. Differentiate between facts and historical interpretations, recognizing that a historian's narrative reflects his or her judgment about the significance of particular facts	**Inquiry Questions:** 1. How does the point of view of the historian impact how history is interpreted? 2. What qualifies an event as historically significant rather than simply noteworthy? 3. What if the history of a war was told by the losing side? 4. Why are historical questions important? 5. How do historical thinkers use primary and secondary sources to formulate historical arguments? 6. How might historical inquiry be used to make decisions on contemporary issues? **Relevance and Application:** 1. Historical information and context are used to interpret, evaluate, and inform decisions or policies regarding such issues as discrimination of various groups – women, indigenous people – throughout history and religious conflicts - the Middle East Peace process, the troubles between the United Kingdom and Northern Ireland, conflicts in Africa and genocide. 2. The historical method of inquiry is used to continue to interpret and refine history. For example, new information and discoveries regarding the origins of the Cold War and new insights into the relationship between Europeans and Africans during the early era of colonization change the interpretation of history. **Nature of History:** 1. Historical thinkers evaluate historical sources for audience, purpose, point of view, context, and authenticity 2. Historical thinkers use primary and secondary sources to evaluate and develop hypotheses and interpretations of historical events and figures

Prepared Graduates:
➢ Analyze key historical periods and patterns of change over time within and across nations and cultures

Grade Level Expectation: High School

Concepts and skills students master:

2. The key concepts of continuity and change, cause and effect, complexity, unity and diversity over time

Evidence Outcomes	21st Century Skills and Readiness Competencies
Students can: World history (both East and West including modern world history): a. Evaluate continuity and change over the course of world history b. Investigate causes and effects of significant events in world history c. Analyze the complexity of events in world history d. Examine and evaluate issues of unity and diversity in world history United States history (Reconstruction to the present): e. Analyze continuity and change in eras over the course of United States history f. Investigate causes and effects of significant events in United States history. Topics to include but not limited to WWI, Great Depression, Cold War g. Analyze the complexity of events in United States history. Topics to include but not limited to the suffrage movement and the Civil Rights Movement h. Examine and evaluate issues of unity and diversity from Reconstruction to present. Topics to include but not limited to the rise and fall of Jim Crow, role of patriotism, and the role of religion	Inquiry Questions: 1. What impact have individuals had on history? 2. How has culture defined civilization? 3. How does society decide what is important in history? 4. What ideas have united people over time? 5. How has diversity impacted the concepts of change over time? Relevance and Application: 1. The complex relationships among change, diversity and unity have long-lasting impacts on the cultural, political, and ideological components in society. For example, there is a need to understand cultural traditions and history in order to interact in the international world of business. 2. The complex interrelationship between the past and the present is evident when solving issues over time. For example, human interaction with the environment has been a critical issue throughout history and continues to be a factor in pollution, climate change, and resource management. 3. Businesses and individuals use history to understand the feasibility of new ideas and markets. Nature of History: 1. Historical thinkers analyze the significance of interactions among eras, ideas, individuals, and groups 2. Historical thinkers organize events into chronological eras and periods 3. Historical thinkers study cause and effect, patterns, themes, and interdependence of events

Prepared Graduates:
➤ Analyze key historical periods and patterns of change over time within and across nations and cultures

Grade Level Expectation: High School

Concepts and skills students master:
3. The significance of ideas as powerful forces throughout history

Evidence Outcomes	21st Century Skills and Readiness Competencies
Students can: World history (both East and West; to include but not be limited to modern world history): a. Discuss the historical development and impact of major world religions and philosophies. Topics to include but not limited to the Enlightenment and modern changes in Christianity, Islam, Judaism, Buddhism and Hinduism b. Investigate the historical development of and impact of major scientific and technological innovations. Topics to include but not limited to the Industrial Revolution c. Evaluate the historical development and impact of political thought, theory and actions d. Analyze the origins of fundamental political debates and how conflict, compromise, and cooperation have shaped national unity and diversity. Topics to include but not limited to suffrage, Civil Rights and the role of government e. Analyze ideas critical to the understanding of American history. Topics to include but not limited to populism, progressivism, isolationism, imperialism, anti-communism, environmentalism, liberalism, fundamentalism, and conservatism f. Describe and analyze the historical development and impact of the arts and literature on the culture of the United States	**Inquiry Questions:** 1. What if the belief "all men are created equal" did not exist? 2. Which ideas provide the greatest insight to understanding a culture or nation's history? 3. How has music, art, and literature reflected powerful ideas throughout history? 4. How have philosophical and religious traditions affected the development of political institutions? 5. How have scientific and technological developments affected societies? **Relevance and Application:** 1. The world is interconnected through the exchange of ideas as evident in science, technology, and economies. Examples include the printing press, trade routes, spread of information through the Internet, scientists working collaboratively but living in different countries, and instant reporting on the Internet. 2. Philosophies, religions, and other powerful ideas have developed over time and across the world. Examples include the spread of religions around the globe, minority rights over time, exploration of space and the oceans, and the Universal Declaration of Human Rights) 3. Literature, art (drama, music, dance) reflect and express powerful ideas over time, such as equal rights, civil disobedience, religious thought and expression, government issues) **Nature of History:** 1. Historical thinkers study and analyze the impacts that arise from the interaction of political, philosophical, technological, artistic, and scientific thought.

Prepared Graduates:
➢ Develop an understanding of how people view, construct, and interpret history

Grade Level Expectation: Eighth Grade

Concepts and skills students master:

1. Formulate appropriate hypotheses about United States history based on a variety of historical sources and perspectives

Evidence Outcomes	21st Century Skills and Readiness Competencies
Students can:	**Inquiry Questions:**
a. Use and interpret documents and other relevant primary and secondary sources pertaining to United States history from multiple perspectives	1. How has the Declaration of Independence influenced other nations?
	2. Which primary documents have had the greatest impact on the people of the United States?
	3. Should and can historians be completely impartial when writing about history?
b. Analyze evidence from multiple sources including those with conflicting accounts about specific events in United States history	4. What makes history different from literature?
	5. Was it "Westward Expansion" or "Territorial Convergence?"
	6. What makes a good historical question?
c. Critique data for point of view, historical context, distortion, or propaganda and relevance to historical inquiry	**Relevance and Application:**
	1. The context and content from the past are used to make connections to the present such as connecting the Civil War to current social and political issues, and the boom and bust cycle of economics with the Gold Rush and railroads
d. Construct a written historical argument on the use or understanding of primary and secondary sources	2. The historical method of inquiry is used to interpret and refine history and serves as a model for inquiry. For example, historians and communities preserve historical documents, artifacts, and buildings.
	Nature of History:
	1. Historical thinkers evaluate historical sources for purpose, audience, point of view, context, and authenticity.
	2. Historical thinkers use primary and secondary sources to evaluate and create hypotheses and interpretations of historical events defended with supporting evidence.

Prepared Graduates:

➢ Analyze key historical periods and patterns of change over time within and across nations and cultures

Grade Level Expectation: Eighth Grade

Concepts and skills students master:

2. The historical eras, individuals, groups, ideas and themes from the origins of the American Revolution through Reconstruction and their relationships with one another

Evidence Outcomes	21st Century Skills and Readiness Competencies
Students can:	**Inquiry Questions:**
a. Determine and explain the historical context of key people and events from the origins of the American Revolution through Reconstruction including the examination of different perspectives	1. How have the basic values and principles of American democracy changed over time and in what ways have they been preserved?
	2. To what extent are the ideas of the American Revolution and the United States Constitution still affecting the world today?
b. Evaluate continuity and change over the course of United States history by examining various eras and determining major sources of conflict and compromise	3. What would the United States be like if the British had won the American Revolution?
	4. To what extent was the Civil War an extension of the American Revolution?
c. Examine factors that motivated the military and economic expansion from the American Revolution through Reconstruction	**Relevance and Application:**
d. Evaluate the impact of different factors – on topics to include but not limited to gender, age, ethnicity and class– on groups and individuals in this time period and the impact of these groups and individuals on the events of the time period	1. The context and information from the past are used to make connections and inform decisions in the present. For example, the concepts of liberty continue to be defended by lawyers and citizens while the rights and responsibilities of citizens continue to evolve through the work of policy makers, legislators, judges, lawyers, and individuals.
e. Analyze causes and effects of major conflicts from the origins of the American Revolution through Reconstruction	2. Technological developments continue to evolve and impact the present. For example, communication media has evolved from printing, telegraph, early photography and continues to continues to evolve, in transportation of scientific discoveries)
f. Analyze ideas that are critical to the understanding of American history and give examples of the ideals involved in major events and movements. Topics to include but not limited to representative democracy, federalism, capitalism, abolition, temperance, nativism, and expansionism	**Nature of History:**
	1. Historical thinkers analyze patterns and themes throughout time.
	2. Historical thinkers study places and events from multiple perspectives in a way that leads to interpretations based on available evidence.
	3. Historical thinkers use chronology to organize time.
	4. Historical thinkers examine sources for audience, purpose, point of view, historical context, and propaganda.

Content Area: Social Studies
Standard: 1. History

Prepared Graduates:
➢ Develop an understanding of how people view, construct, and interpret history

Grade Level Expectation: Seventh Grade

Concepts and skills students master:
1. Seek and evaluate multiple historical sources with different points of view to investigate a
   historical question and to formulate and defend a thesis with evidence

Evidence Outcomes	21st Century Skills and Readiness Competencies
Students can: a. Determine and explain the interdependence of people around the world during significant eras or events b. Analyze historical sources for accuracy and point of view while formulating historical questions. Sources to include but not limited to art, artifacts, eyewitness accounts, letters and diaries, artifacts, real or simulated historical sites, charts, graphs, diagrams, and written texts	Inquiry Questions: 1. Why do people continue to research historical questions and events if books have already been written on the topic? 2. How do historical thinkers defend a thesis using primary and secondary sources that reflect different viewpoints? 3. How and why do historians determine periods of history? 4. What can an artifact tell or not tell about a time period or event? Relevance and Application: 1. Individuals identify points of view, seek multiple sources, and develop and defend a thesis with evidence throughout life. For example, responsible citizens learn about the platforms and beliefs of candidates running for office prior to voting 2. Technology is used to explore and evaluate accuracy of information. For example, editors check stories for accuracy and documentary film makers interview multiple individuals when making a movie. 3. The use the context and content from the past is used to make connections to the present (e.g., the human settlement and trade route patterns) Nature of History: 1. Historical thinkers construct history through the gathering and analysis of historical sources. 2. Historical thinkers construct the story of the past by interpreting events from multiple points of view and various perspectives. 3. Historical thinkers defend a thesis with appropriate resources.

Colorado Department of Education

Adopted: December 10, 2009

Content Area: Social Studies
Standard: 1. History

Prepared Graduates:
➤ Analyze key historical periods and patterns of change over time within and across nations and cultures

Grade Level Expectation: Seventh Grade

Concepts and skills students master:
2. The historical eras, individuals, groups, ideas and themes within regions of the Eastern Hemisphere and their relationships with one another

Evidence Outcomes	21st Century Skills and Readiness Competencies
Students can: a. Explain how people interact and are interconnected over key periods or eras in history in the Eastern Hemisphere b. Determine and explain the historical context of key people, events, and ideas over time and include the examination of different perspectives from people involved c. Describe the foundation and development of key historical topics. Topics to include but not limited to early civilizations, Greece, Rome, ancient China and ancient African civilizations, and the Medieval World incorporating the Crusades and Feudalism d. Analyze the social, political, cultural, economic, and technological development within the topics listed in above in evidence outcome "c" e. Describe the history, interactions, and contributions of various peoples and cultures that have lived in or migrated to the Eastern Hemisphere. Topics to include but not limited to world religions, the Silk Road, East/West contact and settlement patterns	Inquiry Questions: 1. How does the rise or collapse of a government affect surrounding societies over time? 2. What ideas have fundamentally changed different cultures in the Eastern Hemisphere? 3. What are the factors that influenced the development of civilizations and nations? 4. To what extent are ideas from ancient Greece, Rome, China, and Africa important in today's world? Relevance and Application: 1. Historical information and context are used to interpret, evaluate, and inform current decisions or policies. For example, architects use ancient designs to influence their designs and advertisers use historical references in their ads to create context and meaning. 2. Historical philosophies and ideas continue to inform and affect the present. For example, democracy continues to evolve from its Greek origins and cultural traditions change and evolve with global interaction. 3. Technological developments continue to evolve and affect the present. For example, the speed of communication is almost instantaneous with blogs and the Internet. Nature of History: 1. Historical thinkers analyze patterns and themes throughout time. 2. Historical thinkers construct history using a variety of sources. 3. Historical thinkers interpret history from various points of view. 4. Historical thinkers use chronology to organize time. 5. Historical thinkers examine data for point of view, historical context, and propaganda.

Adopted: December 10, 2009

Content Area: Social Studies
Standard: 1. History

Prepared Graduates:
➤ Develop an understanding of how people view, construct, and interpret history

Grade Level Expectation: Sixth Grade

Concepts and skills students master:
1. Analyze and interpret historical sources to ask and research historical questions

Evidence Outcomes	21st Century Skills and Readiness Competencies
Students can: a. Identify ways different cultures record history b. Interpret documents and data from multiple primary and secondary sources while formulating historical questions. Sources to include but not limited to art, artifacts, eyewitness accounts, letters and diaries, artifacts, real or simulated historical sites, charts, graphs, diagrams and written texts c. Critique information to determine if it is sufficient to answer historical questions	**Inquiry Questions:** 1. What questions help us understand the development and interaction of peoples in the Western Hemisphere? 2. How can different sources on the same topic vary and how can we determine which sources are most helpful in interpreting the past? 3. What are the key primary sources that help to understand the history of the Western Hemisphere? 4. How does the author or creator of a source influence the interpretation? **Relevance and Application:** 1. Individuals identify points of view, seek multiple sources, and develop and defend a thesis with evidence throughout life. 2. Technology is used to explore and evaluate for accuracy of information. 3. The context and content from the past is used to make connections to the present. **Nature of History:** 1. Historical thinkers evaluate historical sources for purpose, audience, point of view, context, reliability and authenticity. 2. Historical thinkers use primary and secondary sources to evaluate and develop hypotheses and interpretations of historical events and figures that are supported by evidence.

Content Area: Social Studies
Standard: 1. History

Prepared Graduates:
➤ Analyze key historical periods and patterns of change over time within and across nations and cultures

Grade Level Expectation: Sixth Grade

Concepts and skills students master:

2. The historical eras, individuals, groups, ideas and themes in regions of the Western Hemisphere and their relationships with one another

Evidence Outcomes	21st Century Skills and Readiness Competencies

Evidence Outcomes	21st Century Skills and Readiness Competencies
Students can: a. Explain how people, products, cultures, and ideas interacted and are interconnected over key eras in the Western Hemisphere b. Determine and explain the historical context of key people, events, and ideas over time including the examination of different perspectives from people involved. Topics to include but not limited to Aztec, Maya, Inca, Inuit, early Native American cultures of North America, major explorers, colonizers of countries in the Western Hemisphere, and the Columbian Exchange c. Identify examples of the social, political, cultural, and economic development in key areas of the Western Hemisphere	**Inquiry Questions:** 1. Why have civilizations succeeded and failed? 2. To what extent does globalization depend on a society's resistance to and adaptation to change over time? 3. What factors influenced the development of civilizations and nations? **Relevance and Application:** 1. Historical information and context are used to interpret, evaluate, and inform decisions or policies regarding current issues such as the impact of the Columbian exchange on the world today. 2. Philosophies and ideas from history continue to inform and affect the present such as the Aztec, Maya, and Inca influence. 3. Technological developments continue to evolve and affect the present. For example, the speed of communication is almost instantaneous with blogs and the Internet. **Nature of History:** 1. Historical thinkers analyze patterns and themes throughout time. 2. Historical thinkers study people places, ideas, and events to construct the story of history from multiple perspectives. 3. Historical thinkers use chronology to organize time. 4. Historical thinkers examine data for point of view, historical context, or propaganda.

Content Area: Social Studies
Standard: 1. History

Prepared Graduates:
➢ Develop an understanding of how people view, construct, and interpret history

Grade Level Expectation: Fifth Grade

Concepts and skills students master:

1. Analyze historical sources from multiple points of view to develop an understanding of historical context

Evidence Outcomes	21st Century Skills and Readiness Competencies
Students can: a. Identify different ways of dating historical sources to understand historical context b. Examine significant historical documents. Topics to include but not limited to the Stamp Act, the Declaration of Independence, and the Constitution c. Create timelines of eras and themes in North America from 1491 through the American Revolution d. Analyze cartoons, artifacts, artwork, charts, and graphs related to eras and themes in North America from 1491 through the American Revolution	Inquiry Questions: 1. How do sources with varied perspectives help us to understand what happened in the past? 2. Why is important to understand the historical context of events? 3. How might history be different without the Declaration of Independence? Relevance and Application: 1. Historical information from multiple perspectives is used to interpret, evaluate, and inform; and make decisions and policies regarding various issues. For example, some accounts of the American Revolution refer to American patriots while others refer to American rebels. 2. The historical method of inquiry allows individuals to continue to interpret and refine history. For example, political cartoonists portray multiple perspectives of events, and newspapers may be biased in coverage of events throughout time. Nature of History: 1. Historical thinkers analyze and interpret primary and secondary sources to make inferences about various time periods and show cause-and-effect relationships. 2. Historical thinkers seek people, places, and events that tell the story of history from multiple perspectives. 3. Historical thinkers examine data for point of view, historical context, distortion, or propaganda.

Prepared Graduates:

➢ Analyze key historical periods and patterns of change over time within and across nations and cultures

Grade Level Expectation: Fifth Grade

Concepts and skills students master:

2. The historical eras, individuals, groups, ideas, and themes in North America from 1491 through the founding of the United States government

Evidence Outcomes	21st Century Skills and Readiness Competencies
Students can: a. Identify and explain cultural interactions between 1491 and the American Revolution. Topics to include but not limited to the Columbian Exchange, the interactions between Europeans and native Americans in the 17th and 18th centuries, and the developing relationship between Europeans and enslaved Africans b. Identify and describe the significant individuals and groups of Native Americans and European colonists before the American Revolution c. Explain the development of political, social and economic institutions in the British American colonies d. Explain important political, social, economic, and military developments leading to and during the American Revolution	**Inquiry Questions:** 1. What if Thomas Paine had not written Common Sense? 2. How did historical events and individuals contribute to diversity in the United States? 3. How did important American documents shape American beliefs and values? 4. To what extent did individuals and their ideas contribute to the foundation of the United States government? **Relevance and Application:** 1. The context and information from the past are used to make connections and inform decisions in the present. For example, the concepts of liberty continue to be defended by lawyers and citizens while on topics to include but not limited to the rights and responsibilities of citizens continue to evolve through the work of policy makers, legislators, judges, lawyers, and individuals. 2. Technological developments continue to evolve and affect the present in areas such as communication, transportation, and science. **Nature of History:** 1. Historical thinkers analyze patterns and themes throughout time. 2. Historical thinkers use chronology to organize and study cause-and-effect relationships across time. 3. Historical thinkers study people, places, and events to tell the story of history from multiple perspectives.

Content Area: Social Studies
Standard: 1. History

Prepared Graduates:
➢ Develop an understanding of how people view, construct, and interpret history

Grade Level Expectation: Fourth Grade

Concepts and skills students master:
1. **Organize and sequence events to understand the concepts of chronology and cause and effect in the history of Colorado**

Evidence Outcomes	21st Century Skills and Readiness Competencies
Students can: a. Construct a timeline of events showing the relationship of events in Colorado history with events in United States and world history b. Analyze primary source historical accounts related to Colorado history to understand cause-and-effect relationships c. Explain the cause-and-effect relationships in the interactions among people and cultures that have lived in or migrated to Colorado d. Identify and describe how major political and cultural groups have affected the development of the region	Inquiry Questions: 1. How have past events influenced present day Colorado and the Rocky Mountain region? 2. Why is it important to know the sequence of events and people in Colorado history? 3. How can primary sources help us learn about the past or create more questions about our state's history? 4. What social and economic decisions caused people to locate in various regions of Colorado? Relevance and Application: 1. Individuals recognize important events and can put them in chronological in order to understand cause and effect such as migration west and clashes with Native Americans; discovery of gold and the Gold Rush; the growth of cities and towns and the development of law; the development of the state Constitution; and prohibition of slavery. Nature of History: 1. Historical thinkers analyze patterns and themes throughout time. 2. Historical thinkers use chronology to organize time and to study cause-and-effect relationships. 3. Historical thinkers use primary sources as references for research.

Content Area: Social Studies
Standard: 1. History

Prepared Graduates:
➤ Analyze key historical periods and patterns of change over time within and across nations and cultures

Grade Level Expectation: Fourth Grade

Concepts and skills students master:
2. The historical eras, individuals, groups, ideas and themes in Colorado history and their relationships to key events in the United States

Evidence Outcomes	21st Century Skills and Readiness Competencies
Students can: a. Analyze various eras in Colorado history and the relationship between these eras and eras in United States history, and the changes in Colorado over time b. Describe interactions among people and cultures that have lived in Colorado c. Describe the development of the political structure in Colorado history. Topics to include but not limited to an understanding of the Colorado Constitution and the relationship between state and national government d. Describe the impact of various technological developments. Topics to include but not limited to the state of Colorado, including changes in mining technology; changes in transportation; early 20th century industrial changes; and mid- to late 20th century nuclear and computer technological changes	Inquiry Questions: 1. In what ways have geographic, economic, cultural, and technological changes influenced Colorado today? 2. Why did people of various cultures migrate to and settle in Colorado? 3. To what extent have unity and diversity shaped Colorado? 4. How have various individuals, groups, and ideas affected the development of Colorado? Relevance and Application: 1. The context and information from the past is used to make connections and inform current decisions. For example, Colorado has had a history of boom and bust cycles that should influence the decisions of city and state planners. 2. Technological developments continue to evolve and affect the present. For example, environmental issues have had an impact on Colorado from the Gold Rush to modern pollution. Nature of History: 1. Historical thinkers analyze patterns and themes across time periods. 2. Historical thinkers seek accounts of history from multiple perspectives and from multiple sources.

Adopted: December 10, 2009

Content Area: Social Studies
Standard: 1. History

Prepared Graduates:
➤ Develop an understanding of how people view, construct, and interpret history

Grade Level Expectation: Third Grade

Concepts and skills students master:

1. Use a variety of sources to distinguish historical fact from fiction

Evidence Outcomes	21st Century Skills and Readiness Competencies
Students can: a. Compare factual historical sources with works of fiction about the same topic b. Use a variety of historical sources including artifacts, pictures and documents to help define factual historical evidence c. Compare information from multiple sources recounting the same event	**Inquiry Questions:** 1. How do historical fact, opinion and fiction uniquely influence an individual's understanding of history? 2. How do historical thinkers determine the accuracy of history? 3. What types of questions do historians ask about the past? 4. Why do historians use multiple sources in studying history? **Relevance and Application:** 1. The ability to distinguish fact from fiction is used to make informed decisions. For example, consumers must critically analyze advertisements for facts, and nonfiction writers must verify historical accuracy. 2. The ability to distinguish historical fact from fiction allows local museums and other tourist attractions to relate truthful accounts of the past. **Nature of History:** 1. Historical thinkers evaluate historical sources for purpose and context. 2. Historical thinkers use sources to distinguish fact from fiction.

Colorado Department of Education   Adopted: December 10, 2009

Content Area: Social Studies
Standard: 1. History

Prepared Graduates:
➢ Analyze key historical periods and patterns of change over time within and across nations and cultures

Grade Level Expectation: Third Grade

Concepts and skills students master:
2. People in the past influence the development and interaction of different communities or regions

Evidence Outcomes	21st Century Skills and Readiness Competencies
Students can: a. Compare past and present situations and events b. Chronologically sequence important events in a community or region c. Give examples of people and events, and developments that brought important changes to a community or region d. Describe the history, interaction, and contribution of the various peoples and cultures that have lived in or migrated to a community or region	Inquiry Questions: 1. How have different groups of people both lived together and interacted with each other in the past? 2. What types of questions do people ask to learn about the past? 3. How has the region changed and yet remained the same over time? Relevance and Application: 1. The context and information from the past is used to make connections and inform decisions in the present. For example, the development and traditions of various groups in a region affect the economic development, tourist industry and the cultural make-up of a community. 2. Technological developments continue to evolve and affect the present and permit innovation in a region. For example, Hispanics influence the culture in Pueblo; the military affects the culture in the Pikes Peak region; and the ski industry and mining affect the mountains. Nature of History: 1. Historical thinkers ask questions to guide their research into the past. 2. Historical thinkers analyze the interaction, patterns, and contributions of various cultures and groups in the past.

Colorado Department of Education

Adopted: December 10, 2009

Content Area: Social Studies
Standard: 1. History

Prepared Graduates:

▲ Develop an understanding of how people view, construct, and interpret history

Grade Level Expectation: Second Grade

Concepts and skills students master:

1. Identify historical sources and utilize the tools of a historian

Evidence Outcomes	21st Century Skills and Readiness Competencies
Students can:	Inquiry Questions:
a. Identify community and regional historical artifacts and generate questions about their function and significance	1. How can two people understand the same event differently?
	2. Why is it important to use more than one source for information?
	3. How can putting events in order by time help describe the past?
	4. What kinds of tools and sources do historical thinkers use to investigate the past?
b. Explain the past through oral or written firsthand accounts of history	
c. Explain the information conveyed by historical timelines	Relevance and Application:
d. Identify history as the story of the past preserved in various sources	1. The ability to identify reliable historical sources is essential to searching for and communicating information. For example, individuals searching on the Internet must find reliable sources for information; reporters must find reliable information for news stories; and historians must use scholarly sources when writing nonfiction pieces.
e. Create timelines to understand the development of important community traditions and events	2. The tools of historians are used to share thoughts and ideas about the past such as selecting a historical name for a building, school, park, or playground; recounting a news event in the neighborhood; and using a timeline to gauge progress toward the completion of a project.
	Nature of History:
	1. Historical thinkers gather firsthand accounts of history through oral histories.
	2. Historical thinkers use artifacts and documents to investigate the past.

Prepared Graduates:

➤ Analyze key historical periods and patterns of change over time within and across nations and cultures

Grade Level Expectation: Second Grade

Concepts and skills students master:

2. People have influenced the history of neighborhoods and communities

Evidence Outcomes	21st Century Skills and Readiness Competencies
Students can: a. Organize the historical events of neighborhoods and communities chronologically b. Compare and contrast past and present situations, people, and events in neighborhoods, communities, and the nation c. Give examples of people and events, and developments that brought important changes to the community d. Compare how communities and neighborhoods are alike and different e. Describe the history, interaction, and contribution of the various peoples and cultures that have lived in or migrated to neighborhoods and communities	**Inquiry Questions:** 1. How can understanding the past impact decision-making today? 2. How have events and ideas from the past shaped the identity of communities and neighborhoods today? **Relevance and Application:** 1. Historical information and context are used to interpret, evaluate, and inform decisions or policies regarding current issues. For example, the history of a city determines how it might advertise for tourism purposes. 2. Philosophies and ideas from history continue to inform and impact the present. For example, the independent Western philosophy affects how local government works. 3. Technological developments continue to evolve and affect the present. An example of this would be the way communication is now almost instantaneous and thus, speeds up the nature of events. **Nature of History:** 1. Historical thinkers investigate relationships between the past and present. 2. Historical thinkers organize findings in chronological order as one way to examine and describe the past.

Content Area: Social Studies
Standard: 1. History

Prepared Graduates:
➤ Develop an understanding of how people view, construct, and interpret history

Grade Level Expectation: First Grade

Concepts and skills students master:
1. Describe patterns and chronological order of events of the recent past

Evidence Outcomes	21st Century Skills and Readiness Competencies
Students can: a. Arrange life events in chronological order b. Identify the components of a calendar. Topics to include but not limited to days of the week, months, and notable events c. Identify past events using a calendar d. Use words related to time, sequence, and change	**Inquiry Questions:** 1. Why is it important to know the order of events? 2. How are current patterns similar to and different from those experienced by people who lived in a community in the past? **Relevance and Application:** 1. Events are recorded in sequential order to increase understanding, see relationships, understand cause and effect, and organize information. For example, scientists record information about experiments in sequential order so they can replicate them, and law enforcement re-creates timelines to find missing people or solve crimes. 2. Groups of individuals use similar tools for the organization of sequential information in order to communicate in a clear manner. **Nature of History:** 1. Historical thinkers understand the importance of comparing and contrasting in identifying patterns and trends. 2. Historical thinkers use chronology to sequence events.

Content Area: Social Studies
Standard: 1. History

Prepared Graduates:
➤ Analyze key historical periods and patterns of change over time within and across nations and cultures

Grade Level Expectation: First Grade

Concepts and skills students master:
2. Family and cultural traditions in the United States in the past

Evidence Outcomes	21st Century Skills and Readiness Competencies
Students can: a. Identify similarities and differences between themselves and others b. Discuss common and unique characteristics of different cultures using multiple sources of information c. Identify famous Americans from the past who have shown courageous leadership d. Identify and explain the meaning of American national symbols. Symbols to include but not limited to the American flag, bald eagle, Statue of Liberty, Uncle Sam, the Capitol, and the White House	Inquiry Questions: 1. What are national symbols and their relationship to traditions in the United States? 2. What are family and cultural traditions and how have they changed over time? 3. How have individuals made a difference in their community? Relevance and Application: 1. The understanding of family and cultural traditions informs decisions and creates knowledge that is used throughout life. For example, Uncle Sam is used by political cartoonists to represent the United States. 2. Knowledge of cultural traditions of various groups helps to gain insight, have new experiences, and collaboratively interact with society. For example, bowing is a sign of respect that American businesspersons would use when working in Japan. Nature of History: 1. Historical thinkers understand the importance of comparing and contrasting in identifying patterns and trends. 2. Historical thinkers use chronology to sequence events.

Prepared Graduates:
▲ Develop an understanding of how people view, construct, and interpret history

Grade Level Expectation: Kindergarten

Concepts and skills students master:
1. Ask questions, share information and discuss ideas about the past

Evidence Outcomes	21ˢᵗ Century Skills and Readiness Competencies
Students can: a. Ask questions about the past using question starters. Questions to include but not limited to: What did? Where? When did? Which did? Who did? Why did? How did? b. Identify information from narrative stories that answer questions about the past and add to our collective memory and history c. Use correctly the word "because" in the context of personal experience or stories of the past using words. Words to include but not limited to: past, present, future, change, first, next, last	Inquiry Questions: 1. How are lives of people from the past similar and different from our lives today? 2. Why is it important to ask questions about the past? 3. What is history? Relevance and Application: 1. Individuals identify historical information in stories, photographs, buildings, and documents in their immediate surroundings such as movies, books, poems, paintings and other forms of art. 2. The asking of questions about the past helps to understand the present and plan for the future. For example, newspaper reporters investigate the history of a topic in order to write a well-rounded piece. Nature of History: 1. Historical thinkers ask questions to guide investigations of people, places, and events in the past.

Content Area: Social Studies
Standard: 1. History

Prepared Graduates:
➢ Analyze key historical periods and patterns of change over time within and across nations and cultures

Grade Level Expectation: Kindergarten

Concepts and skills students master:
2. The first component in the concept of chronology is to place information in sequential order

Evidence Outcomes	21st Century Skills and Readiness Competencies
Students can: a. Order sequence information using words. Words to include but not limited to past, present future, days, weeks, months, years, first, next, last, before, and after b. Explore differences and similarities in the lives of children and families of long ago and today c. Explain why knowing the order of events is important	Inquiry Questions: 1. Why is it important to know the order of events? 2. Why do individuals use calendars and clocks? 3. What happened yesterday and today, and what might happen tomorrow? 4. How have you grown and changed over time? Relevance and Application: 1. The recording of events in sequential order helps to create understanding and see relationships, understand cause and effect, and organize information. For example, scientists record information about experiments in sequential order so they can replicate them, and law enforcement re-creates timelines to find missing people. 2. Groups of individuals use similar tools for the organization of sequential information in order to communicate in a clear manner. For example, timelines use standard information such as date, time, month, and year for ease of communication. Nature of History: 1. Historical thinkers use chronology to order information sequentially.

Content Area: Social Studies
Standard: 1. History

Prepared Graduates:
➢ Develop an understanding of how people view, construct, and interpret history

Grade Level Expectation: Preschool

Concepts and skills students master:
  1. Change and sequence over time

Evidence Outcomes	21st Century Skills and Readiness Competencies
Students can: a. Use words and phrases correctly related to chronology and time. Words to include but not limited to past, present future, before, now, and later. b. Select examples from pictures that illustrate past, present, and future c. Sequence a simple set of activities or events d. Identify an example of change over time on topics to include but not limited to their own growth	Inquiry Questions: 1. How have you grown and changed over time? 2. What are important events in your past, your families past, or the past of an adult you know? Relevance and Application: 1. Change occurs over time and has an impact on individuals and society. 2. Sequence and sequencing helps with understanding, such as the sequence of equations in mathematics. 3. Technology is used to record change and sequence. For example, clocks, calendars, and timelines record change. Nature of History: 1. Historical thinkers study and describe past events and change over time in the lives of people. 2. Historical thinkers organize past events using chronology.

2. Geography

[]The study of geography creates an informed person with an understanding of spatial perspective and technologies for spatial analysis; and an awareness of the interdependence of the world regions and resources, and how places are connected at the local, national, and global scales. Students understand the complexity and interrelatedness of people, places, and environments. Geography helps students appreciate the dynamic relationships and complexity of the world.

The skills, concepts, and knowledge acquired in geography are fundamental literacy components for a 21st century student. Use of critical thinking, information literacy, collaboration, self-direction, and invention are apparent in every facet of geographic education. Geography helps students develop a framework for understanding the world, ultimately contributing to the creation of informed citizens.

Prepared Graduates
The prepared graduate competencies are the preschool through twelfth-grade concepts and skills that all students who complete the Colorado education system must master to ensure their success in a postsecondary and workforce setting.

Prepared Graduate Competencies in the Geography standard are:

⋏ Develop spatial understanding, perspectives, and personal connections to the world

⋏ Examine places and regions and the connections among them

Content Area: Social Studies
Standard: 2. Geography

Prepared Graduates:
➤ Develop spatial understanding, perspectives, and personal connections to the world

Grade Level Expectation: High School

Concepts and skills students master:
1. Use different types of maps and geographic tools to analyze features on Earth to investigate and solve geographic questions

Evidence Outcomes	21st Century Skills and Readiness Competencies
Students can: a. Gather data, make inferences and draw conclusions from maps and other visual representations b. Create and interpret various graphs, tables, charts, and thematic maps c. Analyze and present information using a variety of geographic tools and geographic findings in graphs, tables, charts, and thematic maps d. Locate physical and human features and evaluate their implications for society	**Inquiry Questions:** 1. What is the significance of spatial orientation, place, and location? 2. How can maps be used for political purposes? 3. How can current world events change maps? 4. How do the division and control of the physical, social, political, and cultural spaces on Earth cause cooperation or conflict? 5. What would the world map look like if physical geography was the defining variable for country boundaries? **Relevance and Application:** 1. Geographic tools, such as satellite imagery, GIS, GPS, are used to place world events and study human activities over time and provide deeper understanding of the world. For example, satellite imagery is used to track the disappearance of the Aral Sea, find the location of lost cities and measure the melting of ice caps. 2. The location of resources, physical boundaries, and natural hazards affect human interaction such as conflicts over water rights, and location of resources in relation to trade routes and consumers. 3. Technology is used to gather and graph geographic information to inform decisions. For example, weather and climate patterns affect the farming industry, and population and migration patterns affect city planners and Realtors. 4. Technology is used to collect and communicate geographic data such as the distribution of resources and its influence on population density. **Nature of Geography:** 1. Spatial thinkers gather, display, and analyze geographic information using geographic tools. 2. Spatial thinkers use absolute and relative location, mental maps, and spatial orientation in studying geographic questions. 3. Spatial thinkers predict how human activities will help shape Earth's surface and ways that people might cooperate and compete for use of Earth's surface.

Prepared Graduates:

➤ Develop spatial understanding, perspectives, and personal connections to the world

Grade Level Expectation: High School

Concepts and skills students master:

2. Explain and interpret geographic variables that influence the interactions of people, places and environments

Evidence Outcomes	21st Century Skills and Readiness Competencies
Students can: a. Apply geography skills to help investigate issues and justify possible resolutions involving people, places, and environments. Topics to include but not limited to how people prepare for and respond to natural hazards b. Identify, evaluate, and communicate strategies to respond to constraints placed on human systems by the physical environment c. Explain how altering the environment has brought prosperity to some places and created environmental dilemmas for others d. Research and interpret multiple viewpoints on issues that shaped the current policies and programs for resource use e. Explain how information and changing perceptions and values of places and environment influence personal actions f. Define sustainability and explain how an individual's actions may influence sustainability	Inquiry Questions: 1. What will happen if farm land degrades around the world? 2. How might the physical geography of Earth change in the future? 3. Why do countries and cultures struggle to maintain spatial cohesiveness and national identity? 4. What might happen if we thought locally and acted globally? 5. What are the maximum limits of human activity the environment can withstand without deterioration? Relevance and Application: 1. Individual actions affect the local environment and global community such as the impact of recycling and consumption of resources. 2. Technology can support invention and influence how humans modify the environment in both positive and negative ways such as renovation of existing buildings to "green" technologies, prevention and prediction of natural hazards and disasters, and satellite imagery used to track water availability in the Middle East. Nature of Geography: 1. Spatial thinkers study how the physical environment is modified by human activities, including how human societies value and use natural resources. 2. Spatial thinkers evaluate major areas of environmental and societal interaction.

Prepared Graduates:
➤ Examine places and regions and the connections among them

Grade Level Expectation: High School

Concepts and skills students master:
   3. The interconnected nature of the world, its people and places

Evidence Outcomes	21st Century Skills and Readiness Competencies
Students can: a. Explain how the uneven distribution of resources in the world can lead to conflict, competition, or cooperation among nations, regions, and cultural groups b. Explain that the world's population is increasingly connected to and dependent upon other people for both human and natural resources c. Explain how migration of people and movement of goods and ideas can enrich cultures, but also create tensions d. Analyze how cooperation and conflict influence the division and control of Earth e. Analyze patterns of distribution and arrangements of settlements and the processes of the diffusion of human activities f. Make predictions and draw conclusions about the global impact of cultural diffusion	Inquiry Questions: 1. How does increasing globalization influence the interaction of people on Earth? 2. How do cooperation and conflict influence the division and control of the social, economic, and political spaces on Earth? 3. What predictions can be made about human migration patterns? 4. How do technologies result in social change, some of which is unanticipated such as social networking? Relevance and Application: 1. The world is geographically interconnected, affecting daily life in such ways as the spread of disease, global impact of modern technology, and the impact of cultural diffusion. 2. Technology creates new life choices, new interconnections between l people, new opportunities, and new conflicts. For example the spread of knowledge and democratic ideals throughout the world changes lives. Nature of Geography: 1. Spatial thinkers evaluate global systems such as culture, diffusion, interdependence, migration, population pyramids, regional alliances, development of competition and trade, and the impact of population changes on society. 2. Spatial thinkers study the interconnection between physical processes and human activities that help shape the Earth's surface. 3. Spatial thinkers analyze how people's lives and identities are rooted in time and place.

Prepared Graduates:
➤ Examine places and regions and the connections among them

Grade Level Expectation: Eighth Grade

Concepts and skills students master:
1. Use geographic tools to analyze patterns in human and physical systems

Evidence Outcomes	21st Century Skills and Readiness Competencies
Students can:	Inquiry Questions:
a. Interpret maps and other geographic tools as a primary source to analyze a historic issue	1. How has human settlement influenced changes in physical systems and culture?
b. Describe the nature and spatial distribution of cultural patterns	2. How can geographic tools help explore patterns in human and physical systems?
c. Recognize the patterns and networks of economic interdependence	3. How have people and the environment interacted to produce changes over time?
d. Explain the establishment of human settlements in relationship to physical attributes and important regional connections	4. How is human activity limited by the environment?
e. Calculate and analyze population trends	5. How has the environment influenced human activity?
	Relevance and Application:
	1. The analysis and understanding of patterns found in human and physical systems helps to explain impacts on society such as the impact of migration patterns on regions.
	2. Technology is used to find, plot, and express the patterns found in human and physical systems that affect society such as population density and growth analyses, impact of deforestation, and human and environmental changes that affect world health.
	Nature of Geography:
	1. Spatial thinkers use geographic tools to discover and investigate geographic patterns.

Content Area: Social Studies
Standard: 2. Geography

Prepared Graduates:
➤ Develop spatial understanding, perspectives, and personal connections to the world

Grade Level Expectation: Eighth Grade

Concepts and skills students master:
    2. Conflict and cooperation occur over space and resources

Evidence Outcomes	21st Century Skills and Readiness Competencies
Students can: a. Analyze how economic, political, cultural, and social processes interact to shape patterns of human population, interdependence, cooperation and conflict b. Compare how differing geographic perspectives apply to a historic issue c. Interpret from a geographic perspective the expansion of the United States by addressing issues of land, security, and sovereignty	Inquiry Questions: 1. How will the location of resources lead to cooperation or conflict in the future? 2. How has conflict over space and resources influenced human migration? 3. How have differing perspectives regarding resource and land use lead to cooperative policies or conflict? 4. How would human settlement patterns be different if people did not trade resources with others? Relevance and Application: 1. Nations are working cooperatively or are engaged in conflict over the division and control of land, water, and other resources. 2. Individuals and groups make choices regarding the use of space and resources in society. For example, various nations and groups fought over the resources of the United States and businesses and individuals have raced for land and resources throughout history including the Gold Rush and the Western land rush. Nature of Geography: 1. Spatial thinkers study how factors influence the allocation and use of space and resources. 2. Spatial thinkers study how different perspectives affect cooperation and conflict over space and resources.

Prepared Graduates:
➢ Develop spatial understanding, perspectives, and personal connections to the world

Grade Level Expectation: Seventh Grade

Concepts and skills students master:
1. Use geographic tools to gather data and make geographic inferences and predictions

Evidence Outcomes	21st Century Skills and Readiness Competencies
Students can: a. Interpret maps and other geographic tools to find patterns in human and physical systems b. Describe the characteristics and distribution of physical systems, cultural patterns and economic interdependence to make predictions. Topics to include but not limited to environmental issues and cultural diffusion c. Collect and analyze data to make geographic inferences and predictions regarding the Eastern Hemisphere d. Ask and answer questions after examining geographic sources	Inquiry Questions: 1. How would the world be different if we had no maps? 2. How could geographic data be used for both positive and negative results? 3. Why do so many maps of the world put North America in the center? Relevance and Application: 1. Geographic tools and the data they represent help businesses make decisions regarding location such as the best location for a business or the next Olympics. 2. Geography and technology enable the ability to make predictions about such topics as population expansion and need for services. Nature of Geography: 1. Spatial thinkers use geographic tools to discover and investigate geographic patterns. 2. Spatial thinkers use knowledge about the environment to study its influence on individuals and groups.

Content Area: Social Studies
Standard: 2. Geography

Prepared Graduates:
➤ Examine places and regions and the connections among them

Grade Level Expectation: Seventh Grade

Concepts and skills students master:
2. Regions have different issues and perspectives

Evidence Outcomes	21st Century Skills and Readiness Competencies
Students can: a. Classify data to construct thematic maps and make inferences b. Analyze and interpret data using geographic tools and create maps c. Construct maps using fundamental principles to identify key information and analyze regional issues and perspectives in the Eastern Hemisphere d. Explain how the physical environment of a place influences its economy, culture, and trade patterns	Inquiry Questions: 1. Why do geographers use a variety of maps to represent the world? 2. How can a location be in different regions at the same time? 3. How do regional issues affect larger areas? 4. Do regions with similar issues around the world have similar geographic characteristics? Relevance and Application: 1. Individuals and businesses understand the characteristics of a region and its needs. For example, a snowmobile business should not be located in the South and restaurants reflect regional tastes in foods. 2. Regional access to resources affects individual perceptions, what they value, and how they react. For example, water consumption may be based on availability. Nature of Geography: 1. Spatial thinkers study cultural groups in order to explain how they view a region. 2. Spatial thinkers evaluate the use of resources in a region to predict and propose future uses. 3. Spatial thinkers study the various definitions of regions.

Content Area: Social Studies
Standard: 2. Geography

Prepared Graduates:
➢ Develop spatial understanding, perspectives, and personal connections to the world

Grade Level Expectation: Sixth Grade

Concepts and skills students master:

1. Use geographic tools to solve problems

Evidence Outcomes	21st Century Skills and Readiness Competencies
Students can: a. Use longitude, latitude, and scale on maps and globes to solve problems b. Collect and analyze data to interpret regions in the Western Hemisphere c. Ask multiple types of questions after examining geographic sources d. Interpret and communicate geographic data to justify potential solutions to problems e. Distinguish different types of maps and use them in analyzing an issue	Inquiry Questions: 1. How can geographic tools be used to solve problems in the future? 2. How does where we live influence how we live? 3. How do populations, physical features, resources, and perceptions of places and regions change over time? 4. How has land been acquired by countries? 5. How have geographic factors influenced human settlement and economic activity? Relevance and Application: 1. Technology is used by individuals and businesses to answer geographic problems such as the spread of disease, migration patterns, and distribution and loss of resources like water supplies. 2. Geographic tools help to solve problems in daily life. For example, a car GIS is used to find a location, maps are used by tourists, and directions are found on the Internet. Nature of Geography: 1. Spatial thinkers use geographic tools to develop spatial thinking and awareness. 2. Spatial thinkers evaluate patterns that connect people and their problems to the world.

Colorado Department of Education   Adopted: December 10, 2009

Content Area: Social Studies
Standard: 2. Geography

Prepared Graduates:
➤ Examine places and regions and the connections among them

Grade Level Expectation: Sixth Grade

Concepts and skills students master:
2. Human and physical systems vary and interact

Evidence Outcomes	21st Century Skills and Readiness Competencies
Students can: a. Classify and analyze the types of connections between places b. Identify physical features and explain their effects on people in the Western Hemisphere c. Give examples of how people have adapted to their physical environment d. Analyze positive and negative interactions of human and physical systems in the Western Hemisphere	**Inquiry Questions:** 1. What are different ways to define the Western Hemisphere based on human and physical systems? 2. How have people interacted with the environment over time in a positive or negative way? 3. How has globalization affected people and places? 4. In what ways are places on Earth interdependent? **Applying in Society and Using Technology:** 1. The study of how human and physical systems vary and interact helps to make better choices, decisions, and predictions. For example, resource distribution or trade is based on geographic features and environmental changes over time effect a business. 2. Businesses analyze data regarding physical and human systems to make informed choices regarding production, trade, and resource acquisition. 3. Nations use geographic information about human and physical systems to make decisions such as establishing trade routes, locating cities, trade centers and capitals, and establishing outposts and security systems like forts and walls. **Nature of Geography:** 1. Spatial thinkers examine places and regions and the connections among them.

Content Area: Social Studies
Standard: 2. Geography

Prepared Graduates:
➢ Develop spatial understanding, perspectives, and personal connections to the world

Grade Level Expectation: Fifth Grade

Concepts and skills students master:
1. Use various geographic tools and sources to answer questions about the geography of the United States

Evidence Outcomes	21st Century Skills and Readiness Competencies
Students can: a. Answer questions about regions of the United States using various types of maps b. Use geographic tools to identify, locate, and describe places and regions in the United States and suggest reasons for their location c. Locate resources in the United States and describe the influence of access on the development of local and regional communities d. Describe similarities and differences between the physical geography of Colorado and its neighboring states	Inquiry Questions: 1. How can various types of maps and other geographic tools communicate geographic information incorrectly? 2. How do you think differently about data when it is displayed spatially? 3. How and why do we label places? 4. How have places and regions in the United States been influenced by the physical geography of North America over time? Relevance and Application: 1. Geographic tools are used to locate places and identify resources, physical features, regions, and populations. 2. People and organizations decided on specific locations for operations based on geographic information. 3. Technologies enhance the ability to locate and analyze maps to answer questions. For example, historians use maps to help recreate settings of historical events, and individuals use maps to learn about different geographic areas. Nature of Geography: 1. Spatial thinkers recognize that information can be extrapolated from geographic tools. 2. Spatial thinkers evaluate what data and geographic tools are needed to answer specific questions.

Content Area: Social Studies
Standard: 2. Geography

Prepared Graduates:
➤ Examine places and regions and the connections among them

Grade Level Expectation: Fifth Grade

Concepts and skills students master:
2. Causes and consequences of movement

Evidence Outcomes	21ˢᵗ Century Skills and Readiness Competencies
Students can: a. Identify variables associated with discovery, exploration, and migration b. Explain migration, trade, and cultural patterns that result from interactions c. Describe and analyze how specific physical and political features influenced historical events, movements, and adaptation to the environment d. Analyze how cooperation and conflict among people contribute to political, economic, and social divisions in the United States e. Give examples of the influence of geography on the history of the United States	Inquiry Questions: 1. What human and physical characteristics have motivated, prevented, or impeded migration and immigration over time? 2. How can migration and immigration be represented geographically? 3. How has the movement of people and their belongings affected the environment both positively and negatively? Relevance and Application: 1. Individuals understand the consequences and causes of movement to make connections to current personal or international events such as hurricane victims moving from storms, refugees fleeing from war, and economic hardship causing relocation for better jobs. 2. Technology has influenced movement to, colonization of, and the settlement of North America. For example, the West was promoted as the place for economic prosperity. Transportation systems have influenced movement. 3. Migration of individuals has multiple effects on society including economic and environmental impacts. Nature of Geography: 1. Spatial thinkers study patterns of human movement. 2. Spatial thinkers analyze the push and pull components of movement.

Content Area: Social Studies
Standard: 2. Geography

Prepared Graduates:
➢ Develop spatial understanding, perspectives, and personal connections to the world

Grade Level Expectation: Fourth Grade

Concepts and skills students master:
1. Use several types of geographic tools to answer questions about the geography of Colorado

Evidence Outcomes	21st Century Skills and Readiness Competencies	
Students can:	Inquiry Questions:	Relevance and Application:
a. Answer questions about Colorado regions using maps and other geographic tools	1. Which geographic tools are best to locate information about a place?	1. Individuals and businesses learn how to use geographic tools to answer questions about their state and region to make informed choices. For example, a family reads a weather map and researches road conditions to inform their decision to go to the mountains in the winter.
b. Use geographic grids to locate places on maps and images to answer questions	2. Why did settlements and large cities develop where they did in Colorado?	
	3. How are the regions of Colorado defined by geography?	
	4. How does the physical location of Colorado affect its relationship with other regions of the United States and the world?	2. Individuals and businesses use geographic tools to collect and analyze data regarding the area where they live.
c. Create and investigate geographic questions about Colorado in relation to other places		
d. Illustrate, using geographic tools, how places in Colorado have changed and developed over time due to human activity		Nature of Geography:
		1. Spatial thinkers gather appropriate tools to formulate and answer questions related to space and place.
		2. Spatial thinkers use tools to compare and contrast geographic locations.

Colorado Department of Education

Adopted: December 10, 2009

Content Area: Social Studies
Standard: 2. Geography

Prepared Graduates:
➢ Examine places and regions and the connections among them

Grade Level Expectation: Fourth Grade

Concepts and skills students master:
   2. Connections within and across human and physical systems are developed

Evidence Outcomes	21st Century Skills and Readiness Competencies
Students can:	Inquiry Questions:
a. Describe how the physical environment provides opportunities for and places constraints on human activities	1. What physical characteristics led various cultural groups to select the places they did for settlement in Colorado?
	2. How did Colorado settlers alter their environment to facilitate communication and transportation?
b. Explain how physical environments influenced and limited immigration into the state	3. How does the physical environment affect human activity?
	4. How does human activity affect the environment?
c. Analyze how people use geographic factors in creating settlements and have adapted to and modified the local physical environment	Relevance and Application:
	1. Individuals and businesses consider geographic factors in making settlement decisions. For example, Colorado Springs has a dry climate that is favorable for computer companies, and ski resorts developed in the Rocky Mountains.
d. Describe how places in Colorado are connected by movement of goods and services and technology	2. Individuals and businesses adapt to and modify the environment. For example, businesses and resorts have been created near hot springs throughout the state.
	Nature of Geography:
	1. Spatial thinkers evaluate how physical features affect the development of a sense of place.

Colorado Department of Education

Adopted: December 10, 2009

Content Area: Social Studies
Standard: 2. Geography

Prepared Graduates:
➤ Develop spatial understanding, perspectives, and personal connections to the world

Grade Level Expectation: Third Grade

Concepts and skills students master:
1. Use various types of geographic tools to develop spatial thinking

Evidence Outcomes	21st Century Skills and Readiness Competencies
Students can:	Inquiry Questions:
a. Read and interpret information from geographic tools and formulate geographic questions	1. What questions do geographers ask?
	2. How does the geography of where we live influence how we live?
b. Find oceans and continents, major countries, bodies of water, mountains, and urban areas, the state of Colorado, and neighboring states on maps	3. How do physical features provide opportunities and challenges to regions?
	4. How have the cultural experiences of groups in different regions influenced practices regarding the local environment?
c. Locate the community on a map and describe its natural and human features	Relevance and Application:
	1. Individuals and businesses use geographic tools to answer questions about places and locations such as where to locate a business or park, and how to landscape a yard.
d. Identify geography-based problems and examine the ways that people have tried to solve them	2. Spatial thinking involves analysis, problem-solving, and pattern prediction.
	3. Individuals develop spatial thinking to organize and make connections such as reading a map and understanding where you are, where you want to go, and how to get to the destination.
	Nature of Geography:
	1. Spatial thinkers use and interpret information from geography tools to investigate geographic questions.
	2. Spatial thinkers analyze connections among places.

Colorado Department of Education   Adopted: December 10, 2009

Content Area: Social Studies
Standard: 2. Geography

Prepared Graduates:
  ➤ Examine places and regions and the connections among them

Grade Level Expectation: Third Grade

Concepts and skills students master:
  2. The concept of regions is developed through an understanding of similarities and differences in places

Evidence Outcomes	21st Century Skills and Readiness Competencies
Students can: a. Observe and describe the physical characteristics and the cultural and human features of a region b. Identify the factors that make a region unique including cultural diversity, industry and agriculture, and land forms c. Give examples of places that are similar and different from a local region d. Characterize regions using different types of features such as physical, political, cultural, urban and rural	**Inquiry Questions:** 1. Are regions in the world more similar or different? 2. Why do people describe regions using human or physical characteristics? 3. What are geographic characteristics of a region? 4. How do cultures lead to similarities and differences between regions? **Relevance and Application:** 1. Individuals compare and contrast characteristics of regions when making decisions and choices such as where to send children to school, what part of town to live in, what type of climate suits personal needs, and what region of a country to visit. 2. Individuals and businesses make economic, political, and personal decisions such as where to farm, where to locate industry, and where to plant a garden based on geographic characteristics of a region. 3. Individuals and business understand how geography influences the development of rural, urban, and suburban areas. **Nature of Geography:** 1. Spatial thinkers create and use spatial representations of Earth. 2. Spatial thinkers evaluate geographic data and represent it visually.

Content Area: Social Studies
Standard: 2. Geography

Prepared Graduates:
➢ Develop spatial understanding, perspectives, and personal connections to the world

Grade Level Expectation: Second Grade

Concepts and skills students master:

1. Geographic terms and tools are used to describe space and place

Evidence Outcomes	21st Century Skills and Readiness Competencies
Students can: a. Use map keys, legends, symbols, intermediate directions, and compass rose to derive information from various maps b. Identify and locate various physical features on a map c. Identify the hemispheres, equator, and poles on a globe d. Identify and locate cultural, human, political, and natural features using map keys and legends	**Inquiry Questions:** 1. How do you define, organize, and think about the space around you? 2. What is a human feature versus a physical feature? 3. Why do we use geographical tools such as maps, globes, grids, symbols, and keys? 4. How would you describe a setting without using geographic words? 5. How can using the wrong geographic tool or term cause problems? **Relevance and Application:** 1. Individuals use geographic tools and technology such as observations, maps, globes, photos, satellite images, and geospatial software to describe space and uses of space. 2. Individuals and businesses use maps to give directions. **Nature of Geography:** 1. Spatial thinkers use visual representations of the environment. 2. Spatial thinkers identify data and reference points to understand space and place.

Colorado Department of Education

Adopted: December 10, 2009

Content Area: Social Studies
Standard: 2. Geography

Prepared Graduates:
➤ Examine places and regions and the connections among them

Grade Level Expectation: Second Grade

Concepts and skills students master:
2. People in communities manage, modify and depend on their environment

Evidence Outcomes	21st Century Skills and Readiness Competencies
Students can: a. Identify how communities manage and use nonrenewable and renewable resources b. Identify local boundaries in the community c. Explain why people settle in certain areas d. Identify examples of physical features that affect human activity e. Describe how the size and the character of a community change over time for geographic reasons	Inquiry Questions: 1. How do available resources and their uses create change in a community? 2. Are renewable and nonrenewable resources managed well? How do you know? 3. Why are physical features often used as boundaries? 4. What are the various groups in a community and how are they alike and different? 5. How do you choose if you should recycle, reduce, reuse, or throw something away? Relevance and Application: 1. Individuals and businesses understand that they must manage resources in the environment such as conserving water, safeguarding clean air, managing electricity needs, and reducing the amount of waste. 2. Communities collaborate to modify, manage, and depend on the environment. For example, elected officials decide how to manage resources, and communities may limit hunting, water usage, or other activities. 3. Geographic technology is used to gather, track, and communicate how resources might be managed or modified. For example, ski areas track snowfall rates, analyze data for avalanche danger and even create snow. Nature of Geography: 1. Spatial thinkers compare information and data, and recognize that environmental factors influence change in communities. 2. Spatial thinkers study the uneven distribution and management of resources.

Colorado Department of Education

Adopted: December 10, 2009

Content Area: Social Studies
Standard: 2. Geography

Prepared Graduates:
➤ Develop spatial understanding, perspectives, and personal connections to the world

Grade Level Expectation: First Grade

Concepts and skills students master:
   1. Geographic tools such as maps and globes represent places

Evidence Outcomes	21st Century Skills and Readiness Competencies
Students can: a. Explain that maps and globes are different representations of Earth b. Use terms related to directions - forward and backward, left and right – and distance – near and far – when describing locations c. Recite address including city, state, and country and explain how those labels help find places on a map d. Distinguish between land and water on a map or globe e. Create simple maps showing both human and natural features	**Inquiry Questions:** 1. How would an individual describe how to get somewhere without an address? 2. What if we had no geographic tools? 3. How could a flat map truly represent a round globe? 4. Why do people not carry globes to help find their way? **Relevance and Application:** 1. People use geographic terms, tools, and technology in work and play to describe and find places. For example, pilots use maps to make flight plans, hikers use compasses to determine directions, and vacationers use maps to find unfamiliar places. 2. Individuals create and memorize addresses to help locate places. For example, knowing an address is necessary for an ambulance to find it or for an individual to receive mail. **Nature of Geography:** 1. Spatial thinkers use geographic tools to study and represent places.

Content Area: Social Studies
Standard: 2. Geography

Prepared Graduates:
➢ Examine places and regions and the connections among them

Grade Level Expectation: First Grade

Concepts and skills students master:
2. People in different groups and communities interact with each other and with the environment

Evidence Outcomes	21st Century Skills and Readiness Competencies
Students can: a. Identify examples of boundaries that affect family and friends b. Give examples of how people use and interrelate with Earth's resources c. Identify how community activities differ due to physical and cultural characteristics d. Give examples of how schools and neighborhoods in different places are alike and different e. Identify cultural and family traditions and their connections to other groups and the environment	Inquiry Questions: 1. How are places like communities similar to and different from where you live? 2. How do people celebrate traditions? 3. What celebration or tradition would you create? 4. How do people use resources in the local community? 5. How do individuals in the community use the environment? Relevance and Application: 1. Maps change over time. 2. People from various cultures are both similar and different and these differences are reflected in clothing, language, culture influencing social interactions. 3. Boundaries and the need for boundaries affect everyday life. For example, boundary lines determine who owns a piece of property. Nature of Geography: 1. Spatial thinkers study resources, their availability, and use as a key to understanding human interactions with their environment and each other. 2. Spatial thinkers study human and environmental interactions and consequences of those interactions.

Content Area: Social Studies
Standard: 2. Geography

Prepared Graduates:
➤ Examine places and regions and the connections among them

Grade Level Expectation: Kindergarten

Concepts and skills students master:

1. People belong to different groups and live in different places around the world that can be found on a map or globe

Evidence Outcomes	21st Century Skills and Readiness Competencies
Students can: a. Compare and contrast how people live in different settings around the world b. Give examples of food, clothing, and shelter and how they change in different environments c. Distinguish between a map and a globe as ways to show places people live	**Inquiry Questions:** 1. What would it be like to live in another city, state, or country? 2. Why do people belong to different groups? 3. What makes a place special to the people who live there? **Relevance and Application:** 1. People live in different settings and interact with their environment based on location. For example, people living in colder climates wear more clothes, and people in areas where there are floods live on higher ground or in houses on stilts. 2. People belong to different groups throughout their lives including sports teams, hobby clubs, political, or religious groups. **Nature of Geography:** 1. Spatial thinkers investigate other cultures and how they have been influenced by the climate, physical geography, and cultures of an area.

Content Area: Social Studies
Standard: 2. Geography

Prepared Graduates:
➤ Develop spatial understanding, perspectives, and personal connections to the world

Grade Level Expectation: Preschool

Concepts and skills students master:
1. Develop spatial understanding, perspectives, and connections to the world

Evidence Outcomes	21st Century Skills and Readiness Competencies
Students can:	**Inquiry Questions:**
a. Use positional phrasing. Phrases to include but not limited to: over and under, here and there, inside and outside, up and down	1. How do you describe your surroundings? 2. Where is this place located? 3. What would the playground look like if it were organized in a different way? 4. What is a geographical term? 5. What is the importance of location?
b. Identify common places to include but limited to home, school, cafeteria, and gymnasium	**Relevance and Application:**
c. Describe surroundings	1. Specific vocabulary describes space and locations such as the book are under the table, and the pencil is next to the telephone.
d. Use pictures to locate familiar places	2. Words can describe surroundings. For example, the dentist is inside her office; the firefighter is on the truck; and the puppy is inside the doghouse.
e. Use nonlinguistic representations to show understanding of geographic terms	3. Knowledge about location through personal experience integrates geographic terms with spatial thinking.
	4. Individuals perform different activities in different places. For example, cooking is done in the kitchen, hiking in the mountains, walking the dog in the park, learning in school, and working in a store.
	Nature of Geography:
	1. Spatial thinkers investigate other cultures and how they have been influenced by climate, physical geography, and other cultures in an area.
	2. Spatial thinkers understand that space is organized, have personal experiences with their environment, and look for patterns.

Adopted: December 10, 2009

3. Economics

Economics and personal financial literacy teach students the skills, knowledge, and habits that they must master in order to contribute in a positive manner to society. Economics and personal financial literacy teach how to understand personal responsibility, set goals, create plans, evaluate choices, value entrepreneurship, comprehend globalization and international connections, and learn to make rational decisions through critical analysis.

Economics teaches students how society manages its scarce resources, how people make decisions, how people interact in the domestic and international markets, and how forces and trends affect the economy as a whole. Personal financial literacy applies the economic way of thinking to help understand how to manage scarce resources using a logical decision-making process that involves prioritization based on analysis of the costs and benefits of every choice.

Economics and personal financial literacy are essential to function effectively in personal lives, as participants in a global economy, and as citizens contributing to a strong national economy. As citizens, workers, consumers, savers, and investors, members of society must have a level of economic and personal financial literacy that enables them to understand how economies function and to apply economic analysis in their own lives.

Prepared Graduates

The prepared graduate competencies are the preschool through twelfth-grade concepts and skills that all students who complete the Colorado education system must master to ensure their success in a postsecondary and workforce setting.

Prepared Graduate Competencies in the Economics Standard are:

> ➤ Understand the allocation of scarce resources in societies through analysis of individual choice, market interaction, and public policy

> ➤ Acquire the knowledge and economic reasoning skills to make sound financial decisions

Content Area: Social Studies
Standard: 3. Economics

Prepared Graduates:

➢ Understand the allocation of scarce resources in societies through analysis of individual choice, market interaction, and public policy

Grade Level Expectation: High School

Concepts and skills students master:
1. Productive resources – natural, human, capital – are scarce; therefore, choices are made about how individuals, businesses, governments, and societies allocate these resources

Evidence Outcomes	21st Century Skills and Readiness Competencies
Students can: a. Analyze the relationships between economic goals and the allocation of scarce resources b. Explain how economic choices by individuals, businesses, governments, and societies incur opportunity costs c. Understand that effective decision-making requires comparing the additional (marginal) costs of alternatives with the additional (marginal) benefits d. Identify influential entrepreneurs and describe how they have utilized resources to produce goods and services	**Inquiry Questions:** 1. How is marginal thinking used in determining societal and individual decisions? 2. How has globalization changed the availability of human capital? 3. What are some of the ways that the values of a society affect the goods and services it produces? 4. What entrepreneurial idea would solve some of the world scarcity issues? **Relevance and Application:** 1. The availability of natural resources, such as fossil fuels and blood diamonds, has an impact on economic decisions made in a global economy. 2. Entrepreneurship and innovation create new paradigms to address scarcity and choice. Examples include electric cars, cell phones, social networking, Internet, and satellite television. 3. Natural resources can be scarce in the world or specific regions, impacting markets and creating innovation such as projects developed to provide clean drinking water around the world, lack of water in the Middle East created significant desalination research). 4. Marginal thinking allows for good economic decisions to be made by individuals, businesses, and governments. **Nature of Economics:** 1. When using an economic way of thinking individuals study how productive resources are changing in order to anticipate new problems with scarcity of desired resources 2. Economic thinkers analyze how economies utilize resources to meet the cumulative wants and needs of the individuals in a society 3. When using an economic way of thinking individuals study factors that lead to increased economic interdependence, increased productivity, and improved standard of living for the individuals in a society.

Content Area: Social Studies
Standard: 3. Economics

Prepared Graduates:

➤ Understand the allocation of scarce resources in societies through analysis of individual choice, market interaction, and public policy

Grade Level Expectation: High School

Concepts and skills students master:
2. Economic policies affect markets

Evidence Outcomes	21st Century Skills and Readiness Competencies
Students can: a. Analyze how government activities influence the economy. Topics to include but not limited to: taxation, monetary policy, and the Federal Reserve b. Recognize the interaction between foreign and domestic economic policies. Topics to include but not limited to: embargoes, tariffs, and subsidies c. Identify government activities that affect the local, state, or national economy d. Give examples of the role of government in a market economic system e. Analyze how positive and negative incentives influence the economic choices made by individuals, households, businesses, governments, and societies f. Compare and contrast monetary and fiscal policies of the United States government that are used to stabilize the economy	Inquiry Questions: 1. What is government's role in a market economy? 2. How do embargoes and tariffs influence the balance of trade in a positive or negative manner? 3. What is the economic impact of various monetary and fiscal policies that a government can use? 4. How would you change monetary policy? 5. What type of monetary and fiscal policies would be best for businesses? Relevance and Application: 1. Fiscal and monetary policies affect financial markets and individuals such as the impact of exchange rates on tourists, and the effect of interest rates on the cost of borrowing money. 2. Businesses understand and follow the changes in fiscal and monetary policy to make better choices and react to changing markets. 3. Technology allows both individuals and businesses to access up-to-date information regarding fiscal and monetary policies and the fluctuations in markets. 4. Economic behavior is modified based on positive and negative incentives such as tax credits on alternative energy and increases in payroll taxes. Nature of Economics: 1. Economic thinkers gather and analyze data to explore trends and predictions. 2. Economic thinkers study the relationship between policy and market reaction. 3. Economic thinkers decipher trends in financial markets by looking for patterns of behavior.

Content Area: Social Studies
Standard: 3. Economics

Prepared Graduates:
➤ Understand the allocation of scarce resources in societies through analysis of individual choice, market interaction, and public policy

Grade Level Expectation: High School

Concepts and skills students master:
3. Government and competition affect markets

Evidence Outcomes	21st Century Skills and Readiness Competencies
Students can: a. Analyze the role of government within different economies. Topics to include but not limited to command socialism, communism, and market capitalism b. Analyze the role of competition within different market structures. Topics to include but not limited to pure competition, monopolistic competition, oligopoly, and monopoly c. Compare and contrast different economic systems in terms of their ability to achieve economic goals d. Compare and contrast different types of taxing. Topics to include but not limited to progressive, regressive, and proportional	**Inquiry Questions:** 1. In what ways does the United States government influence decisions regarding production and distribution of goods? 2. How does competition affect the choices consumers have in an economy? 3. What are some ways that different market structures affect the goods and services available for purchase? 4. How do various economic systems make decisions regarding production and distribution of goods and the role government will play? **Relevance and Application:** 1. Knowledge of the changing role of government in various markets helps to make informed choices. 2. The understanding of the role of competition in markets helps to make informed decisions and create business strategies. 3. Government taxing and spending policies affect individuals and businesses. **Nature of Economics:** 1. Economic thinkers compare systems of economics to determine how best to meet economic goals. 2. Economic thinkers study the use of monetary and fiscal policies. 3. Economic thinkers analyze the effects of specific government regulations on different groups, including consumers, employees and businesses.

Colorado Department of Education

Adopted: December 10, 2009

Prepared Graduates:

➤ Acquire the knowledge and economic reasoning skills to make sound financial decisions (PFL)

Grade Level Expectation: High School

Concepts and skills students master:

4. Design, analyze, and apply a financial plan based on short- and long-term financial goals (PFL)

Evidence Outcomes	21st Century Skills and Readiness Competencies
Students can: a. Develop a financial plan including a budget based on short- and long-term goals b. Analyze financial information for accuracy, relevance, and steps for identity protection c. Describe factors affecting take-home pay d. Identify sources of personal income and likely deductions and expenditures as a basis for a financial plan e. Describe legal and ethical responsibilities regarding tax liabilities	Inquiry Questions: 1. How can you develop short- and long-term financial goals and plans that reflect personal objectives? 2. How does a consumer determine the accuracy, relevancy, and security of financial information? 3. What is the role that various sources of income play in a financial plan? 4. What are the financial and legal consequences of not paying your taxes? 5. What is the role of education in building financial security? Relevance and Application: 1. Individuals create long- and short-term financial plans that include predictions about education, costs; potential to achieve financial goals; projected income; likely expenditures, savings and interest; credit or loans; and investment decisions including diversification. 2. Individuals are able use the appropriate contracts and identify each party's basic rights and responsibilities to protect financial well-being. 3. Technology allows individuals to research and track information regarding personal finances using such tools as online banking and brokerage accounts. Nature of Economics: 1. Financially responsible individuals describe factors that influence financial planning. 2. Financially responsible individuals plan for tax liabilities. 3. Financially responsible individuals consider opportunity costs of saving over spending and vice versa. 4. Financially responsible individuals analyze economic cycles and make predictions regarding economic trends.

Prepared Graduates:

➤ Acquire the knowledge and economic reasoning skills to make sound financial decisions (PFL)

Grade Level Expectation: High School

Concepts and skills students master:

5. Analyze strategic spending, saving, and investment options to achieve the objectives of diversification, liquidity, income, and growth (PFL)

Evidence Outcomes	21st Century Skills and Readiness Competencies
Students can: a. Compare and contrast the variety of investments available for a diversified portfolio b. Evaluate factors to consider when managing savings and investment accounts c. Explain how economic cycles affect personal financial decisions d. Describe the appropriate types of investments to achieve the objectives of liquidity, income and growth	**Inquiry Questions:** 1. How does a consumer choose between investment options? 2. How might changes in the economic cycle affect future earnings on an individual's investments? 3. What are some ways that you might rate the security, accuracy, and relevancy of financial information? 4. How does compound interest manifest in investment and debt situations? **Relevance and Application:** 1. Investigation of different investment strategies helps to identify which strategies are appropriate for different life stages such as early adulthood through to retirement. 2. The creation of a plan to diversify a portfolio of investments balances risks and returns and prepares for a solid financial future. 3. A personal career plan includes educational requirements, costs, and analysis of the potential job demand to achieve financial well-being. **Nature of Economics:** 1. Financially responsible individuals carefully consider the amount of financial risk that they can tolerate based on life stage and plan for changes in the economic cycles. 2. Financially responsible individuals create plans based on sound economic principles to maximize their standard of living over time.

Prepared Graduates:
➢ Acquire the knowledge and economic reasoning skills to make sound financial decisions (PFL)

Grade Level Expectation: High School

Concepts and skills students master:

6. The components of personal credit to manage credit and debt (PFL)

Evidence Outcomes	21st Century Skills and Readiness Competencies
Students can: a. Analyze various lending sources, services, and financial institutions b. Investigate legal and personal responsibilities affecting lenders and borrowers c. Make connections between building and maintaining a credit history and its impact on lifestyle	**Inquiry Questions:** 1. Why is it important to know the similarities and differences of revolving credit, personal loans, and mortgages? 2. How does the law protect both borrowers and lenders? 3. Why is a good credit history essential to the ability to purchase goods and insurance, and gain employment? 4. When should you use revolving credit and/or personal loans? **Relevance and Application:** 1. The understanding of the components of personal credit allows for the management of credit and debt. For example, individuals can use an amortization schedule to examine how mortgages differ, check a credit history, know the uses of and meaning of a credit score, and use technology to compare costs of revolving credit and personal loans. 2. Knowledge of the penalties that accompany bad credit, such as the inability to qualify for loans, leads to good financial planning. **Nature of Economics:** 1. Financially responsible consumers know their rights and obligations when using credit. 2. Financially responsible consumers frequently check their own credit history to verify its accuracy and amend it when inaccurate. 3. Financially responsible consumers make decisions that require weighing benefit against cost.

Content Area: Social Studies
Standard: 3. Economics

Prepared Graduates:
➢ Acquire the knowledge and economic reasoning skills to make sound financial decisions (PFL)

Grade Level Expectation: High School

Concepts and skills students master:
7. Identify, develop, and evaluate risk-management strategies (PFL)

Evidence Outcomes	21st Century Skills and Readiness Competencies
Students can: a. Differentiate between types of insurance b. Explain the function and purpose of insurance c. Select and evaluate strategies to mitigate risk	**Inquiry Questions:** 1. What are the benefits of car, health, life, mortgage, long-term care, liability, disability, home and apartment insurance? 2. How does a consumer choose between various insurance plans? 3. How does insurance help consumers to prepare for the unexpected? 4. What additional ways can individuals alleviate financial risks? **Relevance and Application:** 1. The knowledge of how to evaluate, develop, revise, and implement risk-management strategies allow individuals to be prepared for the future. For example, a plan for insurance may change over the course of life depending on changing circumstances. 2. Individuals seek advice and counsel from insurance companies, financial planners, and other businesses on risk management. **Nature of Economics:** 1. Financially responsible individuals mitigate the risks associated with everyday life through planning, saving, and insurance. 2. Financially responsible individuals consider insurance as a part of their financial plan.

Adopted: December 10, 2009

Prepared Graduates:

➢ Understand the allocation of scarce resources in societies through analysis of individual choice, market interaction, and public policy

Grade Level Expectation: Eighth Grade

Concepts and skills students master:

1. Economic freedom, including free trade, is important for economic growth

Evidence Outcomes	21st Century Skills and Readiness Competencies	
Students can: a. Give examples of international differences in resources, productivity, and prices that provide a basis for international trade b. Describe the factors that lead to a nation having a comparative and absolute advantage in trade c. Explain effects of domestic policies on international trade d. Explain why nations often restrict trade by using quotas, tariffs, and non-tariff barriers	Inquiry Questions: 1. How do societies benefit from trade and exchange? 2. Why is it important for nations to control trade and exchange? 3. What are the benefits and challenges of trade at the international, national, state, local, and individual levels? 4. How does where and how you purchase products affect the social, economic, and environmental conditions? Relevance and Application: 1. The understanding of trade and collaboration within the market economy is important to business and individual economic success. 2. Analysis of the positive and negative impacts of trade agreements is critical to a nation's economy. For example, the Santa Fe Trail and the opening of trade with Japan in American history. 3. Identification of the role of information as a good or service and its influence on production, trade, income, and technological advances aids businesses to operate efficiently. 4. Innovation and invention create absolute or comparative advantage in trade.	
	Nature of Economics: 1. Economic thinkers explore the patterns and development of the interconnected nature of trade. 2. Economic thinkers analyze the components of economic growth.	

Prepared Graduates:

➤ Acquire the knowledge and economic reasoning skills to make sound financial decisions (PFL)

Grade Level Expectation: Eighth Grade

Concepts and skills students master:

2. Manage personal credit and debt (PFL)

Evidence Outcomes	21st Century Skills and Readiness Competencies
Students can: a. Identify and differentiate between purposes and reasons for debt b. Analyze benefits and costs of credit and debt c. Compare sources of credit d. Describe the components of a credit history	**Inquiry Questions:** 1. Why is understanding credit and debt important? 2. How do you manage debt? 3. Why is it important to know about different types of credit? 4. How do you view debt and credit? 5. When is debt useful? **Relevance and Application:** 1. Technology aids in the research of purchases to find the lowest available cost, compare sources of credit, and track debt. 2. Analysis of the cost of borrowing helps to determine how to manage debt for such items as higher education and automobile purchases. 3. Technology is used to research credit history, credit scores, and the variables that impact a credit history to protect personal financial security. **Nature of Economics:** 1. Financially responsible individuals manage debt. 2. Financially responsible individuals understand the responsibilities associated with the use of credit.

Content Area: Social Studies
Standard: 3. Economics

Prepared Graduates:
➢ Understand the allocation of scarce resources in societies through analysis of individual choice, market interaction, and public policy

Grade Level Expectation: Seventh Grade

Concepts and skills students master:
 1. Supply and demand influence price and profit in a market economy

Evidence Outcomes	21ˢᵗ Century Skills and Readiness Competencies
Students can: a. Define supply and demand b. Identify factors that cause changes in supply and demand c. Define and identify factors that impact price d. Identify examples to illustrate that consumers ultimately determine what is produced in a market economy e. Explain the function of profit in a market economy f. Demonstrate how supply and demand determine equilibrium price and quantity	Inquiry Questions: 1. How do consumers determine what is produced? 2. What happens if a good or service is overpriced? 3. When goods and services are scarce what might happen to price? Why? 4. What happens to price when resources become more plentiful? Relevance and Application: 1. The principle of supply and demand is used to succeed in business. 2. Technology is used as a tool to support global trade in a market economy. For example, bar coding allows companies to keep close track of inventory and sales projections are used to make predictions regarding production. 3. Individual choices affect supply and demand. 4. Natural disasters, politics, financial issues, and trade affect supply and demand. Nature of Economics: 1. Economic thinkers study the effects of local and global supply and demand on the local economy. 2. Economic thinkers study the relationship between local consumers and local and global producers. 3. Economic thinkers investigate consequences and trends related to global trade.

Content Area: Social Studies
Standard: 3. Economics

Prepared Graduates:
► Acquire the knowledge and economic reasoning skills to make sound financial decisions (PFL)

Grade Level Expectation: Seventh Grade

Concepts and skills students master:
2. The distribution of resources influences economic production and individual choices (Economics and PFL)

Evidence Outcomes	21st Century Skills and Readiness Competencies
Students can: a. Give examples that illustrate connections between resources and manufacturing b. Identify patterns of trade between places based on distribution of resources c. Compare and contrast the relative value and different uses of several types of resources d. Use supply and demand analysis to explain how prices allocate scarce goods in a market economy e. Define resources from an economic and personal finance perspective f. Explain the role of taxes in economic production and distribution of resources (PFL) g. Define the various types of taxes students will pay as adults (PFL) h. Demonstrate the impact of taxes on individual income and spending (PFL)	**Inquiry Questions:** 1. How is it advantageous and disadvantageous when a country has valuable resources located within its borders? 2. How does a country acquire resources it does not have? 3. How does the availability or the lack of resources influence production and distribution? 4. What would countries look like without taxes? **Relevance and Application:** 1. Various factors that influence production, including resources, supply and demand, and price (PFL), affect individual consumer choices over time. 2. Technology is used to explore relationships of economic factors and issues related to individual consumers. 3. Analysis of the distribution and location of resources helps businesses to determine business practices such as large companies locating near transportation. **Nature of Economics:** 1. Economic thinkers analyze factors impacting production, distribution, and consumption. 2. Economic thinkers gather data regarding trends in production, use of resources, and consumer choices. 3. Financially responsible individuals understand the purposes of and responsibility to pay various taxes such as property, income and sales.

Colorado Department of Education   Adopted: December 10, 2009

Content Area: Social Studies
Standard: 3. Economics

Prepared Graduates:

➢ Understand the allocation of scarce resources in societies through analysis of individual choice, market interaction, and public policy

Grade Level Expectation: Sixth Grade

Concepts and skills students master:

1. Identify and analyze different economic systems

Evidence Outcomes	21st Century Skills and Readiness Competencies
Students can: a. Describe the characteristic of traditional, command, market, and mixed economic systems b. Explore how different economic systems affect job and career options and the population's standards of living c. Use economic reasoning to explain why certain careers are more common in one region than in another and how specialization results in more interdependence	Inquiry Questions: 1. How do different systems address the production of goods? 2. How are scarce resources distributed in different types of economic systems? 3. How do different economies control the means of production and distribution of goods and services? Relevance and Application: 1. Economic development varies and can be compared across countries in the Western Hemisphere including levels of education and average income. 2. Governments and the private sector in the Western Hemisphere cooperate to distribute goods and services, specialize, and are interdependent in the global economy. 3. Career opportunities are influenced by the type of economic system. Nature of Economics: 1. Economic thinkers study how and why individuals make decisions about purchases. 2. Economic thinkers analyze why different markets develop in different locations. 3. Economic thinkers study the effects of different types of economies on global interdependence.

Content Area: Social Studies
Standard: 3. Economics

Prepared Graduates:

➢ Understand the allocation of scarce resources in societies through analysis of individual choice, market interaction, and public policy

Grade Level Expectation: Sixth Grade

Concepts and skills students master:

2. Saving and investing are key contributors to financial well-being (PFL)

Evidence Outcomes	21st Century Skills and Readiness Competencies
Students can: a. Differentiate between saving and investing b. Give examples of how saving and investing can improve financial well-being c. Describe the advantages and disadvantages of saving for short- and medium-term goals d. Explain the importance of an emergency fund e. Explain why saving is a prerequisite to investing f. Explain how saving and investing income can improve financial well-being	**Inquiry Questions:** 1. Why is it important to save and invest? 2. What types of items would an individual save for to purchase? 3. What are risky investments and why would someone make that type of investment? 4. Why is it important to research and analyze information prior to making financial decisions? **Relevance and Application:** 1. It's important to understand why to save and invest for the future. 2. Technology allows individuals and businesses to track investment earnings. 3. The creation of criteria for us of emergency funds helps to save responsibly. 4. The comparison of returns of various savings and investment options and an adjustment of the investments for good financial decision-making. **Nature of Economics:** 1. Financially responsible individuals manage savings and investments for their financial well-being. 2. Financially responsible individuals understand the risks and rewards associated with investing and saving.

Colorado Department of Education

Adopted: December 10, 2009

Content Area: Social Studies
Standard: 3. Economics

Prepared Graduates:
➢ Understand the allocation of scarce resources in societies through analysis of individual choice, market interaction, and public policy

Grade Level Expectation: Fifth Grade

Concepts and skills students master:
  1. Government and market structures influence financial institutions

Evidence Outcomes	21st Century Skills and Readiness Competencies
Students can: a. Define a capitalist market economy b. Identify governmental activities that affect financial institutions and the economy at the local, state, and national level	Inquiry Questions: 1. Why are there different types of financial institutions? 2. In a market economy, who has the most power? 3. What influence should government have on the economy and financial institutions? Relevance and Application: 1. Knowledge about the role of financial institutions in a market economy allows individuals and businesses to better prepare for financial security. For example, financial analysts monitor the banking industry; individuals can evaluate the services and costs of banking with various institutions; and businesses can borrow money to expand. 2. Government actions affect the services and policies of financial institutions, thereby affecting financial options for individuals. Nature of Economics: 1. Economic thinkers analyze the actions of financial institutions in a market economy.

Content Area: Social Studies
Standard: 3. Economics

Prepared Graduates:
▷ Acquire the knowledge and economic reasoning skills to make sound financial decisions (PFL)

Grade Level Expectation: Fifth Grade

Concepts and skills students master:
2. Use of financial institutions to manage personal finances (PFL)

Evidence Outcomes	21st Century Skills and Readiness Competencies
Students can: a. Identify different financial institutions b. Identify the products and services of financial institutions to include but not limited to: checking accounts, savings accounts, investments, and loans c. Compare and contrast financial institutions, their products, and services	**Inquiry Questions:** 1. What factors are important when establishing savings or investments goals? 2. What risks and benefits are associated with spending versus saving and investing? 3. How can a checking account help to decide how to spend and save? 4. Why do people use financial institutions and not self-banking? 5. How do people choose a financial institution? 6. Why do people need income? **Relevance and Application:** 1. Analysis of the benefits and risks of investing and saving with "virtual" and "brick and mortar" financial institutions helps to make informed financial decisions. 2. Evaluation of the opportunity costs help to make financial decisions. 3. Technology is used to track and graph the interest accrued on a "virtual" investments, checking and savings accounts, investments, and loans. **Nature of Economics:** 1. Financially responsible individuals make informed decisions about saving and investing for short- and long-term goals. 2. Financially responsible individuals research, analyze, and make choices regarding their needs when using financial institutions.

Content Area: Social Studies
Standard: 3. Economics

Prepared Graduates:

➢ Understand the allocation of scarce resources in societies through analysis of individual choice, market interaction, and public policy

Grade Level Expectation: Fourth Grade

Concepts and skills students master:

1. People respond to positive and negative incentives

Evidence Outcomes	21st Century Skills and Readiness Competencies
Students can: a. Define positive and negative economic incentives b. Give examples of the kinds of goods and services produced in Colorado in different historical periods and their connection to economic incentives c. Explain how the productive resources – natural, human, and capital – of Colorado have influenced the types of goods produced and services provided	**Inquiry Questions:** 1. Why are different goods and services important at different times in Colorado's history? 2. How have science and technology changed the economy of Colorado? 3. How have natural, human, and capital resources had both positive and negative impacts on the development of Colorado? **Relevance and Application:** 1. Positive incentives influence behavior predictably over time. For example, responsible individuals save for the future and move for better job opportunities. 2. Negative incentives influence behavior predictably over time. For example, people move or refuse to relocate due to poor climate or resource shortages. 3. Groups use both positive and negative incentives to affect behavior. For example, the tourism industry uses incentives to attract tourists and government agencies use tickets to discourage speeding. and fines for not following regulations **Nature of Economics:** 1. Economic thinkers consider the influence of changing resources and demand on the productivity of a state economy. 2. Economic thinkers study changes in the relationship between the availability of resources and the production of goods and services.

Colorado Department of Education

Adopted: December 10, 2009

Prepared Graduates:
➤ Acquire the knowledge and economic reasoning skills to make sound financial decisions (PFL)

Grade Level Expectation: Fourth Grade

Concepts and skills students master:
2. The relationship between choice and opportunity cost (PFL)

Evidence Outcomes	21st Century Skills and Readiness Competencies
Students can: a. Define choice and opportunity cost b. Analyze different choices and their opportunity costs c. Give examples of the opportunity costs for individual decisions d. Identify risks that individuals face (PFL) e. Analyze methods of limiting financial risk (PFL)	**Inquiry Questions:** 1. What different ways does an individual have to get information when making a decision? 2. How do you know when you've made a good decision? 3. How do you know when you've made a bad decision? **Relevance and Application:** 1. Knowledge of the relationship between choice and opportunity cost leads to good decision-making. For example, a business may have an opportunity to purchase inexpensive land, but the cost may be in the travel time. 2. Decisions are made daily regarding risks such as riding a bicycle, skiing, riding in a car, and spending all of an allowance immediately rather than saving. 3. Businesses make choices about risk. For example, a company locates in a country that has an unstable government or extends credit to individuals. **Nature of Economics:** 1. Economic thinkers analyze opportunity costs associated with making decisions. 2. Economic thinkers analyze data to forecast possible outcomes. 3. Financially responsible individuals understand and categorize the components of risk. 4. Financially responsible individuals mitigate and analyze potential risk.

Prepared Graduates:
➤ Understand the allocation of scarce resources in societies through analysis of individual choice, market interaction, and public policy

Grade Level Expectation: Third Grade

Concepts and skills students master:
   1. Describe producers and consumers and how goods and services are exchanged

Evidence Outcomes	21st Century Skills and Readiness Competencies
Students can: a. Describe the difference between producers and consumers and explain how they need each other b. Describe and give examples of forms of exchange topics to include but not limited to trade and barter c. Describe how the exchange of goods and services between businesses and consumers affects all parties d. Recognize that different currencies and forms of exchange that exist and list the functions of money to include but not limited to such topics as medium of exchange, store of value, and measure of value e. Give examples of how trade benefits individuals and communities and increases interdependency	**Inquiry Questions:** 1. How does an individual know when an exchange benefits both parties? 2. What would happen if there was no such item as money? 3. Would you rather be a producer, consumer, or a mix of both? 4. What happens when a producer cannot make enough to meet consumer demand? 5. What would happen if consumers did not want what a producer made? 6. What would the world look like if there were no transportation that could move goods more than 50 miles? **Relevance and Application:** 1. Production and consumption are essential components of markets and affect everyday life. For example, not enough high-demand toys are produced during Christmas meaning the prices will be higher. Not enough clean drinking water causes higher prices for bottled water. 2. Goods and services are exchanged in multiple ways and are a part of everyday life such as purchasing or trading items. 3. Production, consumption, and the exchange of goods and services are interconnected in the world. For example, vegetables from California are sold at a Colorado markets and an ice storm in Florida affects orange juice supplies for the world, ingredients from different areas of the United States are shipped to one area for a business to create a candy bar which is then shipped throughout the world. **Nature of Economics:** 1. Economic thinkers analyze trade and the use of money. 2. Economic thinkers describe and study the importance of exchange in a community.

Content Area: Social Studies
Standard: 3. Economics

Prepared Graduates:
➤ Acquire the knowledge and economic reasoning skills to make sound financial decisions (PFL)

Grade Level Expectation: Third Grade

Concepts and skills students master:
2. Describe how to meet short term financial goals (PFL)

Evidence Outcomes	21st Century Skills and Readiness Competencies
Students can: a. Identify sources of income including gifts, allowances, and earnings b. Recognize that there are costs and benefits associated with borrowing to meet a short-term financial goal c. Identify jobs children can do to earn money for personal, philanthropic, or entrepreneurial goals d. Create a plan for a short-term financial goal e. Describe the steps necessary to reach short-term financial goals	**Inquiry Questions:** 1. What would happen if an individual spent all earning on entertainment? 2. Why do individuals give away money? 3. How would an individual decide between purchasing a want or a need? **Relevance and Application:** 1. Personal financial goal setting is a lifelong activity and short-term goal setting is essential to that process. For example, students save for a fish aquarium or skateboard. 2. Analysis of various options and creating short- and long-term goals for borrowing is a lifelong skill. For example, adults borrow to buy a car or a vacation. **Nature of Economics:** 1. Financially responsible individuals create goals and work toward meeting them. 2. Financially responsible individuals understand the cost and the accountability associated with borrowing.

Adopted: December 10, 2009

Content Area: Social Studies
Standard: 3. Economics

Prepared Graduates:

➤ Understand the allocation of scarce resources in societies through analysis of individual choice, market interaction, and public policy

Grade Level Expectation: Second Grade

Concepts and skills students master:
1. The scarcity of resources affects the choices of individuals and communities

Students can:	21st Century Skills and Readiness Competencies
a. Explain scarcity b. Identify goods and services and recognize examples of each c. Give examples of choices people make when resources are scarce d. Identify possible solutions when there are limited resources and unlimited demands	**Inquiry Questions:** 1. How does scarcity affect purchasing decisions? 2. What goods and services do you use? 3. How are resources used in various communities? 4. What are some ways to find out about the goods and services used in other communities? **Relevance and Application:** 1. Comparison of prices of goods and services in relationship to limited income helps to make informed and financially sound decisions. 2. Decisions must be made if there is a limited amount of income and the need for a costly good or service. For example, you may borrow, save, or get a new job to make the purchase. (PFL) 3. Scarcity of resources affects decisions such as where to buy resources based on cost or where to locate a business. **Nature of Economics:** 1. Economic thinkers analyze how goods and services are produced and priced. 2. Economic thinkers analyze scarcity of resources and its impact on cost of goods and services.

Content Area: Social Studies
Standard: 3. Economics

Prepared Graduates:
➤ Acquire the knowledge and economic reasoning skills to make sound financial decisions (PFL)

Grade Level Expectation: Second Grade

Concepts and skills students master:
2. Apply decision-making processes to financial decisions (PFL)

Evidence Outcomes	21st Century Skills and Readiness Competencies
Students can: a. Identify components of financial decision-making including gathering, evaluating, and prioritizing information based on a financial goal, and predicting the possible outcome of a decision b. Differentiate between a long-term and a short-term goal	**Inquiry Questions:** 1. How do individuals make and analyze the consequences of financial decisions? 2. How do individuals meet their short- and long-term goals? **Relevance and Application:** 1. Personal financial decisions are based on responsible evaluation of the consequences. 2. Purchase decisions are based on such things as quality, price, and personal goals. For example, you decide whether to spend money on candy or the movies. **Nature of Economics:** 1. Financially responsible individuals use good decision-making tools in planning their spending and saving.

Content Area: Social Studies
Standard: 3. Economics

Prepared Graduates:
➤ Understand the allocation of scarce resources in societies through analysis of individual choice, market interaction, and public policy

Grade Level Expectation: First Grade

Concepts and skills students master:
1. People work at different types of jobs and in different types of organizations to produce goods and services and receive an income

Evidence Outcomes	21st Century Skills and Readiness Competencies	
Students can: a. Give examples of different types of business and the goods and services they produce for the community b. Give examples of types of jobs people in your family have c. Recognize that people have a choice about what kinds of jobs they do	**Inquiry Questions:** 1. What kinds of jobs do people that you know perform? 2. Where do they go to do those jobs? 3. Why do people choose different jobs? 4. What do workers receive for their work? 5. What types of businesses are in the community? 6. What is the difference between income and money?	
	Relevance and Application: 1. Different forms of technology are used to perform jobs such as scanners for the market checkers, GIS for geographers, machines for industrial work, and computers in offices. 2. Individuals make decisions about careers or jobs based on factors such as education, skills, and interests.	
	Nature of Economics: 1. Economic thinkers investigate the influence of different jobs and businesses in their community. 2. Economic thinkers study the choices about what kinds of jobs people perform.	

      Adopted: December 10, 2009

Content Area: Social Studies
Standard: 3. Economics

Prepared Graduates:
➤ Acquire the knowledge and economic reasoning skills to make sound financial decisions (PFL)

Grade Level Expectation: First Grade

Concepts and skills students master:
2. Identify short-term financial goals (PFL)

Evidence Outcomes	21st Century Skills and Readiness Competencies
Students can: a. Define a short-term financial goal b. Identify examples of short-term financial goals c. Discuss sources of income needed to meet short-term goals such as but not limited to gifts, borrowing, allowances, and income	**Inquiry Questions:** 1. How does an individual earn money to meet a goal? 2. Why do people donate to charity? 3. How does an individual know a good short-term goal? 4. Why is personal financial goal setting important? **Relevance and Application:** 1. Short-term financial goals can be met through planning. For example, an individual divides income between current expenses, saving for the future, and philanthropic donations. 2. Individuals and organizations track their progress toward meeting short-term financial goals. For example, the food bank creates a chart tracking how much food has been donated toward reaching its goal. **Nature of Economics:** 1. Financially responsible individuals create goals and work toward meeting them. 2. Financially responsible individuals understand the cost and the accountability associated with borrowing.

Content Area: Social Studies
Standard: 3. Economics

Prepared Graduates:
➢ Understand the allocation of scarce resources in societies through analysis of individual choice, market interaction, and public policy

Grade Level Expectation: Kindergarten

Concepts and skills students master:
  1. Ownership as a component of economics

Evidence Outcomes	21st Century Skills and Readiness Competencies
Students can: a. Give examples of ownership of different items b. Recognize and give examples one person may want to use another's object and that this requires asking permission and sharing	Inquiry Questions: 1. Can you show me who owns this (any item)? 2. If you want to use someone else's item what must you do? 3. What happens when someone wants to use something that belongs to you? 4. What do we do if there is not enough of something we all want? (scarcity) 5. What are things that everyone collectively owns? Relevance and Application: 1. Individuals interact with each other and the concept of ownership on a daily basis. For example, people purchase items for their use, donate items for others to use, and ask for permission to use someone else's item. 2. Technology is used to indicate and keep track of ownership. For example, pets may have microchips implanted and libraries use bar codes to keep track of their books. Nature of Economics: 1. Economic thinkers study ownership as a key principle of economics. 2. Economic thinkers understand that some items are more desired than others and are more in demand.

Content Area: Social Studies
Standard: 3. Economics

Prepared Graduates:
➢ Acquire the knowledge and economic reasoning skills to make sound financial decisions (PFL)

Grade Level Expectation: Kindergarten

Concepts and skills students master:
2. Discuss how purchases can be made to meet wants and needs (PFL)

Evidence Outcomes	21st Century Skills and Readiness Competencies
Students can: a. Identify the difference between personal wants and needs b. Give examples of the difference between spending income on something you want versus something you need	**Inquiry Questions:** 1. What are wants and needs? 2. How do people balance between wants and needs? 3. What is the difference between a want and a need? 4. How can money help people to meet their wants and needs? **Relevance and Application:** 1. Individuals make choices about purchasing to serve wants and needs. For example, parents pay bills prior to purchasing movie tickets or toys. **Nature of Economics:** 1. Financially responsible individuals differentiate between needs and wants.

Prepared Graduates:

➢ Understand the allocation of scarce resources in societies through analysis of individual choice, market interaction, and public policy

Grade Level Expectation: Preschool

Concepts and skills students master:

1. People work to meet wants and needs

Evidence Outcomes	21st Century Skills and Readiness Competencies
Students can:	Inquiry Questions:
a. Explain that people work (produce) for an income	1. What might happen if no one worked?
b. Discuss that money is used to buy items that the student or family wants	2. What do we buy and why?
c. Give examples to distinguish spending from saving	3. How do people use income?
	4. Why do you save income?
	Relevance and Application:
	1. Working enables people to meet wants. For example, a parent works to receive income used to purchase items such as food, cars and vacations.
	Nature of Economics:
	1. Economic thinkers analyze the connection between working and earning income.
	2. Economic thinkers recognize that people use income to meet needs and wants.

Content Area: Social Studies
Standard: 3. Economics

Prepared Graduates:
➤ Acquire the knowledge and economic reasoning skills to make sound financial decisions (PFL)

Grade Level Expectation: Preschool

Concepts and skills students master:
  2. Recognize money and identify its purpose (PFL)

Evidence Outcomes	21st Century Skills and Readiness Competencies
Students can: a. Recognize coins and currency as money b. Identify how money is used as a medium of exchange c. Discuss why we need money	Inquiry Questions: 1. Why do people use money? 2. What are the different forms of money? Relevance and Application: 1. Recognition of units of money aids in making purchases. For example, a parent pays for an item using correct change. 2. Knowledge of coins and currency ensures accurate transactions. For example, you can check that a cashier gave you the right amount of change. 3. Money is a medium of exchange. Nature of Economics: 1. Financially responsible individuals use money wisely.

Adopted: December 10, 2009

4. Civics

Civics has an impact on every individual daily through the work of city councils, state legislatures, Congress and school boards. Civics teaches students the complexity of the origins, structure, and functions of governments; the rights, roles, and responsibilities of ethical citizenship; the importance of law; and the skills necessary to participate in all levels of government.

Civics is a foundational component of the educational experience and critical to the continued success of our society. A democratic and free society relies on the skills, intelligence, engagement and virtue of its citizens. Our students will one day be responsible for strengthening our civic culture based on the knowledge they learn at school, their own values, and their choices for action. Democracy demands that they have these tools to be responsible contributors to civic culture.

Prepared Graduates

The prepared graduate competencies are the preschool through twelfth-grade concepts and skills that all students who complete the Colorado education system must master to ensure their success in a postsecondary and workforce setting.

Prepared Graduate Competencies in the Civics standard are:

> ➤ Analyze and practice rights, roles, and responsibilities of citizens
>
> ➤ Analyze the origins, structure, and functions of governments and their impacts on societies and citizens

Adopted: December 10, 2009

Content Area: Social Studies
Standard: 4. Civics

Prepared Graduates:
➢ Analyze and practice rights, roles, and responsibilities of citizens

Grade Level Expectation: High School

Concepts and skills students master:
1. Research, formulate positions, and engage in appropriate civic participation to address local, state, and national issues or policies

Evidence Outcomes	21st Century Skills and Readiness Competencies
Students can: a. Engage ethically in civic activities including discussing current issues, advocating for their rights and the rights of others, practicing their responsibilities, influencing governmental actions, and other community service learning opportunities b. Evaluate how individuals and groups can effectively use the structure and functions of various levels of government to shape policy c. Describe the roles and influence of individuals, groups, and the press as checks on governmental practices d. Identify which level of government is appropriate for various policies and demonstrate an ability to appropriately engage with that level of government e. Critique various media sources for accuracy and perspective	**Inquiry Questions:** 1. What is the meaning of civic participation in a democratic republic? 2. How do citizens act as a "check" on government? 3. What strategies can citizens use most effectively to influence public policy? 4. How do people resolve differences while remaining respectful of multiple perspectives? 5. Why should you participate in government? **Relevance and Application:** 1. Decision-making involves researching an issue, listening to multiple perspectives, and weighing potential consequences of alternative actions. For example, citizens study the issues before voting. 2. Participation in a local or national issue involves research, planning, and implementing appropriate and ethical civic engagement. For example, citizens speak at a school board meeting or run for office. 3. Technology is a tool for researching civic issues, advocating for ideas, and expressing views to elected officials. **Nature of Civics:** 1. Responsible community members research civic issues and act appropriately using a variety of sources from multiple perspectives and communicating views in a respectful, ethical manner.

Prepared Graduates:

➤ Analyze origins, structure, and functions of governments and their impacts on societies and citizens

Grade Level Expectation: High School

Concepts and skills students master:

2. Purposes of and limitations on the foundations, structures and functions of government

Evidence Outcomes	21st Century Skills and Readiness Competencies
Students can:	**Inquiry Questions:**
a. Describe the origins, purposes and limitations of government and include the contribution of key philosophers and documents	1. What are the most important democratic ideals and practices?
	2. What would society look like if several landmark court cases had been decided differently?
b. Identify the structure, function, and roles of members of government and their relationship to democratic values	3. How does government best protect individual rights and the rights of minorities, yet have the majority rule?
c. Analyze and explain the importance of the principles of democracy and the inherent competition among values. Values to include but not be limited to freedom and security, individual rights and common good, and rights and responsibilities	4. What would United States government look like with no checks and balances or another mix of those limitations?
	Relevance and Application:
	1. Skills and strategies are used to participate in public life and exercise rights, roles, and responsibilities. For example, eligible individuals vote, individuals pay taxes to support government services, and citizens act as advocates for ideas.
d. Analyze the role of the founding documents and the evolution of their interpretation through governmental action and court cases. Documents to include but not limited to the United States Constitution and the Bill of Rights	2. Political issues are covered by the media, and individuals evaluate multiple media accounts using technology.
e. Use media literacy skills to locate multiple valid sources of information regarding the foundations, structures, and functions of government	**Nature of Civics:**
	1. Responsible community members understand the concept of "rule of law" and its role in policies and practices of the government.
f. Analyze how court decisions, legislative debates, and various and diverse groups have helped to preserve, develop, and interpret the rights and ideals of the American system of government	2. Responsible community members know the political theories that contributed to the foundation and development of the structures of government and their meaning today.
g. Evaluate the effectiveness of our justice system in protecting life, liberty, and property	

Content Area: Social Studies
Standard: 4. Civics

Prepared Graduates:
➤ Analyze origins, structure, and functions of governments and their impacts on societies and citizens

Grade Level Expectation: High School

Concepts and skills students master:
3. Analyze how public policy - domestic and foreign - is developed at the local, state, and national levels and compare how policy-making occurs in other forms of government

Evidence Outcomes	21st Century Skills and Readiness Competencies
Students can: a. Discuss multiple perspectives on local issues and options for participating in civic life b. Analyze and discuss multiple perspectives on state issues and option for participating in civic affairs by shaping policies c. Explain how to monitor and influence public policy d. Analyze goals and tools used by the United States in developing foreign policy e. Illustrate how various governments and leaders interact and evaluate how interactions among nations affect domestic and world events f. Compare and contrast how different systems of government function	Inquiry Questions: 1. Why do countries view global issues from different perspectives? 2. How does domestic policy affect foreign policy? 3. How does a government make foreign policy and can individuals influence policy decisions? 4. What are possible motivations underlying foreign policy decisions? Relevance and Application: 1. The making of foreign and domestic policies impacts daily lives. For example, unrest in the Middle East could cause gasoline prices to rise and unrest in another nation affects extended families in the United States. Nature of Civics: 1. Responsible community members gather and analyze data from multiple sources to look for patterns and create hypotheses regarding foreign policy. 2. Responsible community members investigate foreign policy issues prior to making decisions.

Prepared Graduates:

➤ Analyze and practice rights, roles, and responsibilities of citizens

Grade Level Expectation: Eighth Grade

Concepts and skills students master:

1. Analyze elements of continuity and change in the United States government and the role of citizens over time

Evidence Outcomes	21st Century Skills and Readiness Competencies
Students can: a. Describe instances in which major political, social, economic, or cultural changes occurred and the reasons for the changes b. Analyze the changing definition of citizenship and give examples of the expansion of rights c. Describe examples of citizens and groups who have influenced change in United States government and politics d. Evaluate the result of various strategies for political change over time e. Analyze primary sources supporting democratic freedoms and the founding of our government. Documents to include but not limited to the Declaration of Independence, Constitution, Bill of Rights and explain how they provide for both continuity and change f. Examine ways citizens may effectively voice opinions, monitor government, and bring about change nationally	**Inquiry Questions:** 1. What is a patriot? 2. What are the various roles of government? 3. How have various people from different eras in our nation's history promoted change in the face of opposition and what democratic principles were advanced? 4. How have the meanings of American ideals remained the same and changed over time? **Relevance and Application:** 1. There are elements that contribute to continuity and change in order to maintain a free and democratic society. For example, the right to vote is fundamental in society, but who can vote has changed over time. 2. Individuals work collaboratively to research and advocate ideas regarding important issues facing society such as suffrage, the rights of workers, and the rights of children. **Nature of Civics:** 1. Responsible community members read diverse sources to create understanding, critically analyze issues, and place them in historical context. 2. Responsible community members understand and discuss the dynamic nature of national government and the individual's role in the process.

Content Area: Social Studies
Standard: 4. Civics

Prepared Graduates:
➤ Analyze origins, structure, and functions of governments and their impacts on societies and citizens

Grade Level Expectation: Eighth Grade

Concepts and skills students master:
2. The place of law in a constitutional system

Evidence Outcomes	21st Century Skills and Readiness Competencies
Students can: a. Discern various types of law b. Evaluate the strengths and weaknesses of rule of law c. Describe and engage in various means of conflict management d. Explain the role and importance of the Constitution e. Discuss the tensions between individual rights, state law, and national law f. Explain how state and federal court power of judicial review is reflected in the United States form of constitutional government g. Use a variety of resources to identify and evaluate issues that involve civic responsibility, individual rights, and the common good	Inquiry Questions: 1. What is the "common good?" 2. What are key court cases and historical events in the development of the United States? 3. What are examples of successful and unsuccessful conflict resolution in United States history and why? 4. How has the United States balanced individual rights and law? 5. Which is more effective, the rule of law or the rule of man? Why? Relevance and Application: 1. Laws interact and may remain the same or change over time. For example, in a society with laws, leadership can change but the law remains the same. 2. Laws allow understanding of the proper course of action and consequences for not adhering to the law. For example, safety belts are required in automobiles for safety reasons and various government agencies regulate industries to protect the common good. Nature of Civics: 1. Responsible community members exercise their rights and responsibilities to effect change. 2. Responsible community members understand rule of law and judicial review as components of the judicial system.

Adopted: December 10, 2009

Content Area: Social Studies
Standard: 4. Civics

Prepared Graduates:
➢ Analyze origins, structure, and functions of governments and their impacts on societies and citizens

Grade Level Expectation: Seventh Grade

Concepts and skills students master:
1. Compare how various nations define the rights, responsibilities, and roles of citizens

Evidence Outcomes	21st Century Skills and Readiness Competencies
Students can: a. Compare the definition of citizen in various governments b. List the responsibilities of citizens in various governments c. Define the roles of citizens in various governments d. Give national and international examples of ethics and quality in government policies and practices e. Give examples illustrating how various governments and citizens interact and analyze how these interactions have changed over time	Inquiry Questions: 1. What are fundamental human rights? 2. How can the definition of citizen change? 3. What is the purpose of government? 4. What roles of citizens are the most important? Relevance and Application: 1. The comparison of how different nations define the rights, responsibilities and roles of their citizens helps to understand the actions and reactions of various nations and their citizens to current events. For example, groups in France and Italy freely demonstrate while demonstrations in China are less frequent. Nature of Civics: 1. Responsible community members exercise their rights, responsibilities, and roles. 2. Responsible community members understand that rights, responsibilities, and roles of citizens are different over time and in various nations.

Content Area: Social Studies
Standard: 4. Civics

Prepared Graduates:
➢ Analyze and practice rights, roles, and responsibilities of citizens

Grade Level Expectation: Seventh Grade

Concepts and skills students master:
2. Different forms of government and international organizations and their influence in the world community

Evidence Outcomes	21st Century Skills and Readiness Competencies
Students can:	**Inquiry Questions:**
a. Compare different forms of government in the world and how they derive their authority	1. How do international laws and organizations help encourage ethical governmental practices?
b. Evaluate how various nations interact, resolve their differences, and cooperate	2. How do the aggressive actions of a nation influence other nations and international organizations?
	3. What leads to cooperation, competition, or aggression between and among nations?
c. Analyze conflicts among nations including causes and consequences	4. Why do governments form alliances and join international organizations?
d. Describe common interests and evaluate examples of global collaboration	**Relevance and Application:**
e. Use criteria that identify the attributes of a good government and apply to specific examples	1. The use of technology to research how various countries, their governments, and nongovernmental organizations work collaboratively to solve issues allows global participation in advocacy for beliefs. For example, scientists from different nations work together to help solve the global warming issues and charitable organizations send aid to areas of need.
	2. International organizations influence the world community to contribute or protect beliefs and interests. For example, the European Union was created for economic reasons, and the International Committee of the Red Cross was created to support people in crisis.
	Nature of Civics:
	1. Responsible community members know the components of various systems of government.
	2. Responsible community members develop criteria to apply standards of ethics and quality in evaluating the effectiveness of government.
	3. Responsible community members understand the connections and complexities of interactions among nations.

Prepared Graduates:
➢ Analyze and practice rights, roles, and responsibilities of citizens

Grade Level Expectation: Sixth Grade

Concepts and skills students master:
1. Analyze the interconnectedness of the United States and other nations

Evidence Outcomes	21st Century Skills and Readiness Competencies
Students can: a. Discuss advantages and disadvantages of living in an interconnected world b. Examine changes and connections in ideas about citizenship in different times and places c. Describe how groups and individuals influence the government and other nations d. Explain how political ideas and significant people have interacted, are interconnected, and have influenced nations e. Analyze political issues from both a national and global perspective over time f. Identify historical examples illustrating how Americans from diverse backgrounds perceived and reacted to various global issues	**Inquiry Questions:** 1. What does it mean to live in an interconnected world? 2. How can you be a productive member of the global community and a contributing citizen of the United States? 3. Why are there greater challenges and opportunities when multiple groups interact? 4. Why are national and global viewpoints sometimes different? **Relevance and Application:** 1. Nations are interconnected and affect each other on a daily basis. For example, businesses are affected by the laws, regulations, nations and markets are damaged by drought, earthquakes and other natural disasters throughout the world. 2. Technology provides daily information regarding the interaction between the United States government and other nations. **Nature of Civics:** 1. Responsible community members discuss and analyze how various government decisions impact people, places, and history. 2. Responsible community members analyze how the actions of individuals and groups can have a local, nation, and international impact. 3. Responsible community members analyze the relationship between rights and responsibility in national and global contexts.

Content Area: Social Studies
Standard: 4. Civics

Prepared Graduates:
➤ Analyze origins, structure, and functions of governments and their impacts on societies and citizens

Grade Level Expectation: Sixth Grade

Concepts and skills students master:
2. Compare multiple systems of government

Evidence Outcomes	21st Century Skills and Readiness Competencies

Students can:
 	
a. Describe different forms of government
 	
b. Identify how different forms of government relate to their citizens. Topics to include but limited to democracy and authoritarian government
 	
c. Compare the economic components of different forms of government
 	
d. Compare various governments' and the liberties of their citizens
	Inquiry Questions:
	  1. How do you define good government?
	  2. What evidence can you find of effective and ineffective governments in the past and the present?
	  3. What would a government look like if you created it?
	  4. What are the consequences if a government does not provide for the common good?
	
	Relevance and Application:
	  1. The ability to understand the different forms of government affects daily life. For example, employees work in international corporations and tourists visit countries with different laws, rules, and regulations.
	  2. Knowledge of government is essential for understanding the implications of events around the world.
	
	Nature of Civics:
	  1. Responsible community members discuss personal and national actions and their global consequences.
	  2. Responsible community members identify ways in which lives are enriched and challenged because of the interconnected nature of a global society.

Colorado Department of Education   Adopted: December 10, 2009

Content Area: Social Studies
Standard: 4. Civics

Prepared Graduates:
➤ Analyze and practice rights, roles, and responsibilities of citizens

Grade Level Expectation: Fifth Grade

Concepts and skills students master:
 1. The foundations of citizenship in the United States

Evidence Outcomes	21st Century Skills and Readiness Competencies
Students can: a. Describe and provide sources and examples of individual rights b. Give examples of group and individual actions that illustrate civic ideals in the founding of the United States. Ideals to include but not limited to freedom, rules of law, equality, civility, cooperation, respect, responsibility, and civic participation c. Explain the reasons for the settlement of the American colonies d. Define the criteria and process for becoming a citizen	**Inquiry Questions:** 1. How might citizens view an issue differently because of their backgrounds? 2. What is the most important right of a citizen? 3. What is the most important responsibility of a citizen? 4. How does government meet its responsibility to citizens? 5. Who is government? **Relevance and Application:** 1. Actions illustrate civic virtues such as civility, cooperation, respect, and responsible participation and are foundational components of our society. Examples include peaceful assembly by groups and respectful behavior during a performance or speech. 2. Knowledge of the foundations of citizenship in the United States ensures that citizens' rights are being protected. For example, the rule of law applies to everyone in society and all individuals and groups are treated with respect. **Nature of Civics:** 1. Responsible community members analyze critical historical documents to investigate the development of the national government. 2. Responsible community members understand the responsibilities of the national government to its citizens.

Content Area: Social Studies
Standard: 4. Civics

Prepared Graduates:
➢ Analyze origins, structure, and functions of governments and their impacts on societies and citizens

Grade Level Expectation: Fifth Grade

Concepts and skills students master:
2. The origins, structure, and functions of the United States government

Evidence Outcomes	21st Century Skills and Readiness Competencies
Students can: a. Identify political principles of American democracy and how the Constitution and Bill of Rights reflect and preserve these principles b. Explain the historical foundation and the events that led to the formation of the United States constitutional government. Topics to include but not limited to the colonial experience, the Declaration of Independence, and the Articles of Confederation c. Explain the origins, structure, and functions of the three branches of the United States government and the relationships among them d. Describe how the decisions of the national government affect local and state government	**Inquiry Questions:** 1. What are democratic ideals and practices and their historic origins? 2. Were the founding fathers correct in keeping the Constitution open for flexibility and interpretation? Why? 3. How have historical documents defined and distributed power? **Relevance and Application:** 1. The origins, structure, and function of the United States government are studied to create an informed, civically literate, and responsible society. For example, fundamental principles and liberties are still evolving as judges interpret the Constitution, and legislators make laws and local city councils and boards create regulations **Nature of Civics:** 1. Responsible community members understand the concept of individual rights as a cornerstone to American democracy. 2. Responsible community members understand the relationships between individual rights and personal responsibility.

Colorado Department of Education   Adopted: December 10, 2009

Content Area: Social Studies
Standard: 4. Civics

Prepared Graduates:
➢ Analyze and practice rights, roles, and responsibilities of citizens

Grade Level Expectation: Fourth Grade

Concepts and skills students master:
    1. Analyze and debate multiple perspectives on an issue

Evidence Outcomes	21st Century Skills and Readiness Competencies
Students can: a. Give examples of issues faced by the state and develop possible solutions b. Provide supportive arguments for both sides of a current public policy debate c. Discuss how various individuals and groups influence the way an issue affecting the state is viewed and resolved	Inquiry Questions: 1. How can government answer questions about issues in a state in various ways? 2. How do diverse opinions enrich a community? 3. How does an individual's experience and background influence perception of an issue? 4. Why is it important to research issues and engage in civil debates? Relevance and Application: 1. The art of debate, critical reasoning, and active listening are skills that foster informed choices. For example, school boards review the pros and cons of an issue such as dress code and make a policy decision. 2. The ability to critically analyze multiple perspectives for solutions allows for improved problem-solving. For example, members of a social organization review multiple proposals to select a philanthropic cause for the year. Nature of Civics: 1. Responsible community members recognize opportunities to study the effectiveness of various ways to influence state public policy or help industry create an environmentally conscious development. 2. Responsible community members understand the relationships between state government and citizens.

Content Area: Social Studies
Standard: 4. Civics

Prepared Graduates:
➤ Analyze origins, structure, and functions of governments and their impacts on societies and citizens

Grade Level Expectation: Fourth Grade

Concepts and skills students master:
2. The origins, structure, and functions of the Colorado government

Evidence Outcomes	21st Century Skills and Readiness Competencies
Students can: a. Explain the origins, structure, and functions of the three branches of the state government and the relationships among them b. Identify and explain a variety of roles leaders, citizens, and others play in state government c. Identify and explain the services state government provides and how those services are funded d. Explain the historical foundation and the events that led to the formation of the Colorado government e. Describe how the decisions of the state government affect local government and interact with federal law	Inquiry Questions: 1. Why is Colorado's Constitution important to individuals? 2. What would state government look like if one of the branches had more power than the others? 3. What would Colorado be like without a state government? 4. To what extent were various individuals and organizations in the state important in the development of Colorado's government? Relevance and Application: 1. Knowledge of the origins, structure, and functions of Colorado's government provides for participation, influence and benefits. For example, individuals can vote on ballot issues that affect taxes. 2. Technology helps to investigate resources and ask for government support and services. For example, someone wanting to open a restaurant can visit the Department of Health website to get information. Nature of Civics: 1. Responsible community members understand the structure, function, and origin of the state government.

Colorado Department of Education

Adopted: December 10, 2009

Prepared Graduates:
➤ Analyze and practice rights, roles, and responsibilities of citizens

Grade Level Expectation: Third Grade

Concepts and skills students master:
1. Respecting the views and rights of others is a key component of a democratic society

Evidence Outcomes	21st Century Skills and Readiness Competencies
Students can: a. Identify and apply the elements of civil discourse elements to include but not limited to listening with respect for understanding and speaking in a respectful manner b. Identify important economic and personal rights and how they relate to others c. Give examples of the relationship between rights and responsibilities	**Inquiry Questions:** 1. Why might an individual make a choice to participate in the community? 2. What are the essential elements of compromise that enable conflict to be transformed into agreement? 3. Why is personal advocacy important in a community with diverse views? 4. What would a community be like if individuals from various groups did not respect each other's rights and views? **Relevance and Application:** 1. Respect for the views of others helps to learn and understand various perspectives, thoughts, and cultures. For example, environmentalists, industry, and government work together to solve issues around energy and other resources. 2. Technology provides the opportunity to research multiple views on issues to better understand the evolution of rights. For example, lawyers research court findings and individuals engage in civic discourse regarding issues of the day through the Internet. **Nature of Civics:** 1. Responsible community members take the opportunity to make positive changes in their community. 2. Responsible community members recognize the value of respecting the rights and views of others.

Prepared Graduates:
➤ Analyze origins, structure, and functions of governments and their impacts on societies and citizens

Grade Level Expectation: Third Grade

Concepts and skills students master:
2. The origins, structure, and functions of local government

Evidence Outcomes	21st Century Skills and Readiness Competencies
Students can: a. Identify the origins, structure, and functions of local government b. Identify and explain the services local governments provide and how those services are funded c. Identify and explain a variety of roles leaders, citizens, and others play in local government	**Inquiry Questions:** 1. How are local governments and citizens interdependent? 2. How do individuals get involved in their local government? 3. How do local governments and citizens help each other? 4. Why do people create governments? 5. How do people, places, and events help us understand the ideals of democratic government? **Relevance and Application:** 1. Knowledge of the origins, structure, and functions of local government enables participation in the democratic process. For example, groups and governments work together to create a safe environment in the community. **Nature of Civics:** 1. Responsible community members are involved in their local government. 2. Responsible community members know how personal advocacy and involvement can lead to change in communities. 3. Responsible community members use negotiation as an inherent part of decision-making.

Content Area: Social Studies
Standard: 4. Civics

Prepared Graduates:
➤ Analyze and practice rights, roles, and responsibilities of citizens

Grade Level Expectation: Second Grade

Concepts and skills students master:
1. Responsible community members advocate for their ideas

Evidence Outcomes	21st Century Skills and Readiness Competencies
Students can:	Inquiry Questions:
a. List ways that people express their ideas respectfully	1. What are beliefs that help people live together in communities?
b. Identify how people monitor and influence decisions in their community	2. What civic responsibilities do you think are important?
c. Describe ways in which you can take an active part in improving your school or community	3. How can different cultures and beliefs influence a community?
	4. What are responsible ways to advocate ideas in a community?
d. Identify and give examples of civic responsibilities that are important to individuals, families, and communities	Relevance and Application:
e. Describe important characteristics of a responsible community member	1. Ideas are promoted through the use of various media such as blogs, websites, flyers, and newsletters.
	2. Individuals collaborate to responsibly advocate for the ideas they think will improve society. For example, a group lobbies the city council to create a new park or employ more firefighters.
	Nature of Civics:
	1. Responsible community members influence the rules, policies, and law in their communities.

Content Area: Social Studies
Standard: 4. Civics

Prepared Graduates:
➤ Analyze origins, structure, and functions of governments and their impacts on societies and citizens

Grade Level Expectation: Second Grade

Concepts and skills students master:
2. People use multiple ways to resolve conflicts or differences

Evidence Outcomes	21st Century Skills and Readiness Competencies
Students can: a. Give examples of ways that individuals, groups, and communities manage conflict and promote equality, justice, and responsibility b. Identify examples of power and authority and strategies that could be used to address an imbalance, including bullying as power without authority c. Identify and give examples of appropriate and inappropriate uses of power and the consequences d. Demonstrate skills to resolve conflicts or differences	**Inquiry Questions:** 1. What happens when someone uses power unwisely? 2. What are good ways to solve differences? 3. What would it be like if everyone was friends? 4. What do equality, justice, and responsibility look like in the world? **Relevance and Application:** 1. Conflict can arise for many reasons, including lack of information, or value or personality differences, and conflict may be resolved through compromise, competition, collaboration or avoidance. For example, parents may compromise about where to live. 2. Various forms of conflict resolution are used to solve conflicts and differences. For example, city councils may call for a public hearing to learn what the community thinks about a new jail or library. **Nature of Civics:** 1. Responsible community members know democratic and undemocratic principles and practices and how they are used in diverse communities. 2. Responsible community members examine how culture influences the disposition of rules, laws, rights, and responsibilities. 3. Responsible community members understand that power and authority shape individual participation.

Content Area: Social Studies
Standard: 4. Civics

Prepared Graduates:
➢ Analyze and practice rights, roles, and responsibilities of citizens

Grade Level Expectation: First Grade

Concepts and skills students master:
    1. Effective groups have responsible leaders and team members

Evidence Outcomes	21st Century Skills and Readiness Competencies
Students can: a. Describe the characteristics of responsible leaders b. Identify the attributes of a responsible team member c. Demonstrate the ability to be both a leader and team member	**Inquiry Questions:** 1. How do you know if you are a responsible team member? 2. How do you know if you are a responsible leader? 3. What qualities make a responsible leader and can they change? 4. How do you know when you are working with an effective team? **Relevance and Application:** 1. Groups work as a team toward a collective goal that honors the views of its members. For example, a family decides to save money toward a vacation or a student cleans the house to help the family. 2. Good leadership skills involve being able to plan, collaborate, investigate, listen, and problem solve. For example, teachers listen to the needs of students when trying to make a decision about what is best for the class and a student is able to help mediate a conflict between two friends. **Nature of Civics:** 1. Responsible community members know how to be a good leader and good team member.

Content Area: Social Studies
Standard: 4. Civics

Prepared Graduates:
➤ Analyze origins, structure, and functions of governments and their impacts on societies and citizens

Grade Level Expectation: First Grade

Concepts and skills students master:
   2. Notable people, places, holidays and patriotic symbols

Evidence Outcomes	21st Century Skills and Readiness Competencies
Students can: a. Give examples of notable leaders of different communities leaders to include but not limited to the president, mayor, governor, and law enforcement b. Give examples of various patriotic symbols to include but not limited to the flag, bald eagle, Uncle Sam, and the national anthem c. Identify significant places. Places to include but not limited to the Statue of Liberty, Capitol, White House, and important community sites d. Identify significant civic holidays e. Identify the American flag and the Colorado flag	Inquiry Questions: 1. Why do we have national, community, and local celebrations and holidays? 2. Who are important people in the development of our country? 3. How are new national symbols, songs, or holidays created? Relevance and Application: 1. Symbols, songs, holidays, traditions, places, and people help to provide identity for the community and nation. For example, the Pledge of Allegiance is said on various occasions, individuals may salute the flag of their country, and patriotic songs are sung at sporting events and July 4th parades celebrate our nation's independence. Nature of Civics: 1. Responsible community members understand the responsibilities of being a member of a community. 2. Responsible community members see communities as multi-dimensional entities. 3. Responsible community members investigate responsibility as a central part of group membership.

Prepared Graduates:

➤ Analyze origins, structure, and functions of governments and their impacts on societies and citizens

Grade Level Expectation: Kindergarten

Concepts and skills students master:
1. Participate in making decisions using democratic traditions

Evidence Outcomes	21st Century Skills and Readiness Competencies		
Students can: a. Explain why rules are needed b. Create and follow classroom rules c. Explain how a class rule promotes fairness and resolves conflict d. Contribute to making and maintaining class community decisions e. Give examples of the difference between democratic voting and decisions made by authorities including but not limited to the parent, teacher, or principal	**Inquiry Questions:** 1. What would it look like to have no rules? 2. How can we solve conflict in a fair manner? 3. Why do we consider voting fair?	**Relevance and Application:** 1. Rules help to ensure a safe society. For example, everyone wears seat belts in the car and games have rules to create fairness. 2. Decisions are made cooperatively. For example, families vote on which movie to see and classes vote to see what project they will do.	**Nature of Civics:** 1. Responsible community members take an active role in their communities. 2. Responsible community members know the importance of participation in democratic societies. 3. Responsible community members know the importance of fairness and conflict resolution.

Prepared Graduates:

➢ Analyze origins, structure, and functions of governments and their impacts on societies and citizens

Grade Level Expectation: Kindergarten

Concepts and skills students master:

2. Civic participation takes place in multiple groups

Evidence Outcomes	21st Century Skills and Readiness Competencies
Students can: a. Categorize examples of people and events that relate to civic participation b. Give examples of qualities of a good citizen c. Practice citizenship skills including courtesy, honesty, and fairness in working with others	**Inquiry Questions:** 1. What qualities make people good citizens? 2. Why would people want to have friends from different groups? 3. What can you do to be an active and helpful member of your class and school? **Relevance and Application:** 1. The ability for civic participation differs with age and place. For example, children can volunteer and adults can run for elected office. 2. Individual actions can make the community better. For example, people clean up the highways or volunteer in shelters. **Nature of Civics:** 1. Responsible community members exist across the globe and participation is influenced by cultural norms. 2. Responsible community members study citizen participation and structures that bring security and stability to community life.

Adopted: December 10, 2009

Content Area: Social Studies
Standard: 4. Civics

Prepared Graduates:
➤ Analyze and practice rights, roles, and responsibilities of citizens

Grade Level Expectation: Preschool

Concepts and skills students master:
1. Individuals have unique talents and work with others in groups

Evidence Outcomes	21st Century Skills and Readiness Competencies
Students can: a. Recognize membership in family, neighborhood, school, team, and various other groups and organizations b. Name groups to which they belong and identify the leader(s) c. Identify examples of times when people can play different roles and bring unique talents to a variety of groups	**Inquiry Questions:** 1. What makes an individual unique? 2. Why would a person want to belong to a group? 3. How can differences among group members make groups better? **Relevance and Application:** 1. People join groups based on similar interests and talents such as dance groups, Boy Scouts, or play groups 2. Groups have common purposes such as cleaning up a street, helping students learn, or playing a sport. 3. There are different roles in groups including leaders and team members. **Nature of Civics:** 1. Responsible community members know the roles of individuals vary by the purpose of the group. 2. Responsible community members identify qualities of leadership and effective action.

Colorado Department of Education   Adopted: December 10, 2009

Content Area: Social Studies

Standard: 4. Civics

Prepared Graduates:

➤ Analyze origins, structure, and functions of governments and their impacts on societies and citizens

Grade Level Expectation: Preschool

Concepts and skills students master:

2. Rules and their purpose in allowing groups to work effectively

Evidence Outcomes	21st Century Skills and Readiness Competencies
Students can: a. Explain that groups have rules b. Recognize interpersonal boundaries c. Exert self-control d. Interact positively with others e. Give examples of some rules that are permanent and some that change	Inquiry Questions: 1. What happens when people do not work cooperatively? 2. What personal boundaries are common? 3. What happens if there are no rules? Relevance and Application: 1. Actions affect us and others. For example, fighting may result in injury and punishment. 2. Rules are different in different settings. For example, school rules may be different from home rules. 3. Situations may be fairer because of rules such as taking turns on playground equipment. Nature of Civics: 1. Responsible community members identify the effects of rules on individuals and groups. 2. Responsible community members investigate the causes of inequities that exist within and among groups. 3. Responsible community members study the tension between preserving security, and order and liberty.

Colorado Department of Education
Office of Standards and Assessments
201 East Colfax Ave. • Denver, CO 80203 • 303-866-6929
www.cde.state.co.us

CPSIA information can be obtained at www.ICGtesting.com
Printed in the USA
LVOW05s0042110114

368937LV00002B/55/P